# THE RETURN OF THE PRIMITIVE

Drawing on psychoanalysis, and on literature in the Christian tradition that has for many centuries focused on dreams and visions, Richard Fenn presents a new cross-disciplinary theory of religion. Reflecting that religious language must recover sources of the Christian tradition that have long explored the more primitive aspects of the psyche, the author examines dreams, visions of the afterlife, and descents into hell in the search for a contemporary spiritual discipline. Whereas earlier Christian ascetic practices reinforced the sense of the individual's ultimate helplessness to achieve spiritual maturity, Fenn argues that the psychoanalytic tradition offers a riskier method whose outcome is correspondingly more hopeful and less certain. At the very least, this contemporary descent into hell holds out the promise of a new selfhood that can place certain perennial spiritual struggles in the past.

This book sheds new light on the conflict between psychoanalysis and religion, as well as the nature of modernity and notions of the sacred. It will prove of particular value not only to students and scholars in the psychology or sociology of religion, but more generally to all who are concerned with spirituality, secularization, and the Sacred.

*'This book is about what it means to call one's soul one's own. It is no mere repetition of other positions but an incisive analysis of human self-understanding and self-deception from a deeply humane and scholarly perspective. With its interdisciplinary commitment, this book will intrigue numerous scholars of religion from Patristic theologians to anthropologists.'*

Douglas Davies, University of Durham, UK

*'In his latest book, Richard Fenn explores the unity of social and psychic life through the "excluded possibilities" that shadow identity. While the task of religion today must be to regain the "language of the soul", Fenn goes further – he is a guide to secular descent, death and desire – still the crucible of the human. Once again, Fenn is erudite, provocative, personal.'*

Catherine Bell, Santa Clara University, USA

D1329921

# THEOLOGY AND RELIGION IN INTERDISCIPLINARY PERSPECTIVE SERIES

## Series Editors

Professor Douglas Davies, University of Durham, UK
Professor Richard Fenn, Princeton Theological Seminary, New Jersey, USA

Creativity through shared perspectives lies at the heart of Ashgate's new series on Theology and Religion in Interdisciplinary Perspective. Central religious and theological topics can be raised to a higher order of expression and clarity when approached through interdisciplinary perspectives; this new series aims to provide a pool of potential theories and worked-out examples as a resource for ongoing debate, fostering intellectual curiosity rather than guarding traditional academic boundaries and extending, rather than acting as a simple guide to, an already well-defined field. Major theological issues of contemporary society and thought, as well as some long-established ideas, are explored in terms of current research across appropriate disciplines and with an international compass. The books in the series will prove of particular value to senior undergraduates, graduate and postgraduates, individual academics and others who see the benefit to be derived from bringing together ideas and information that often exist in relative isolation.

# The Return of the Primitive

A New Sociological Theory of Religion

RICHARD K. FENN
*Princeton Theological Seminary, USA*

# Ashgate

Aldershot • Burlington USA • Singapore • Sydney

Published by
Ashgate Publishing Limited
Gower House
Croft Road
Aldershot
Hants GU11 3HR
England

Ashgate Publishing Company
131 Main Street
Burlington VT 05401-5600 USA

Ashgate website: http://www.ashgate.com

**British Library Cataloguing in Publication Data**

Fenn, Richard K.
  The return of the primitive: a new sociological theory of religion.
  – (Theology and religion in interdisciplinary perspective)
  1. Religion and sociology
  I. Title
  306.6

**Library of Congress Cataloging-in-Publication Data**

Fenn, Richard K.
  The return of the primitive: a new sociological theory of religion / Richard K. Fenn.
    p. cm. – (Theology and religion in interdisciplinary perspective)
    ISBN 0–7546–0419–5 — ISBN 0–7546–0420–9 (pbk.)
      1. Religion and sociology. 2. Psychoanalysis and religion. I. Title. II. Series.

BL60 .F44 2001
306.6–dc21

2001022640

ISBN 0 7546 0419 5 (Hbk)
ISBN 0 7546 0420 9 (Pbk)

Typeset by The Midlands Book Typesetting Company, Loughborough.
Printed and bound in Great Britain by MPG Books Ltd., Bodmin, Cornwall.

# Contents

# Acknowledgements

Several friends and colleagues have been particularly helpful in reading and criticizing earlier drafts of this manuscript. David Martin, Linda Woodhead, Paul Heelas and Douglas Davies have been very supportive, and their criticisms have spurred me to make several revisions. Alex Wright's interest in the manuscript was also immensely supportive at an early stage in the writing. As always, James Moorhead and Don Capps have been sympathetic and encouraging in many ways that sustain what has inevitably been a very personal project.

I wish to thank Marianne Delaporte, a graduate student and research assistant at Princeton Theological Seminary, for her work in directing me to a number of the sources used in this book, primarily the early medieval visions and the recent discussions of dreaming in late antiquity.

At Ashgate, the editor, Sarah Lloyd, has been patient and steadfast in her support for this project, and her confidence that I would carry it through has been more than sustaining. I have also relied on the good offices of Barbara Pretty, who has cheerfully and faithfully seen the book into print.

I dedicate this book to my dear wife Cally.

Richard Fenn

*For Cally*

# Introduction

No one, neither shamans nor the Central Intelligence Agency, can know all the possibilities that face a particular society. Even if one could probe within a society to its very depths as well as survey its environment for every possible affiliation and alliance, one would be unable to see every possibility for sedition or treason, for enlightenment or salvation. One would still have to admit that many such possibilities are simply beyond the range of current intelligence and imagination. As it is with the social environment, so it is with nature: there are microbes that have not yet been imagined, let alone discovered, and aliens from outer space that may come, if they come at all, in forms that have yet to be conceived.

The problem is not merely that one's experience is limited, although that is always true and warrants caution. Neither is the problem simply that one's perceptions are distorted, although I think an attitude of suspicion toward one's perceptions is usually preferable to naïveté in that regard. Nor is the problem simply that one's knowledge is always flawed in some respect, although it is better to be skeptical than innocent in making claims to know what one is talking about. The problem is that any system, social or psychological, and thus every society and person, requires a vast reduction in what can be imagined, let alone experienced, perceived, understood and explained. For instance, many societies claim that they represent some sort of an improvement on other societies or on nature itself precisely because they exclude certain possibilities on the basis that what is excluded is underdeveloped, unworthy or even barbaric: that is, relatively 'primitive.' The indigenous population, the old country, or certain aliens and – in the realm of nature – various forms of animal behavior often seem underdeveloped or, in the case of animals, sub-human. Whether or not they are imagined to be friendly, they are considered primitive in the sense of being aboriginal: present, as it were, at the beginnings of life but long since outgrown, superseded or overcome.

To put it another way, societies and persons exist as such to the extent that they can construe certain possibilities as belonging to the past, no matter how recurrent or inviting these possibilities may actually still be. That is why hell, as we shall see, exists alongside a society but only in the past tense. Once it is released from the past, of course, hell may enter the future in the form of the apocalypse. That is why so many versions of hell have been written in the form of apocalyptic warnings or of visions of a much-to-be dreaded future.[1] The world as it is, of course, is far beyond what we can know; we can only imagine it. There are microbial and atomic forces that shape and destroy us, of which we have as yet only a partial knowledge. There are ideas and ideologies that seem at times to be a 'clear and present danger' to a society that has at best only a limited knowledge of its own inner potentiality for deviance and subversion. There are also real, not merely imaginary, antagonists and rivals that threaten to explode bombs or distribute poisons against which many societies and persons as yet have no defenses at all. I will say more about these external sources of danger and uncertainty in the first chapter, on the subject of how societies understand and imagine the 'primitive.' Here it is enough to know that any society creates a world of the primitive by what it places beyond the pale of its own knowledge, control and way of life.

What is beyond the borders of a civilization has long been considered barbaric or primitive. Have not Western societies defined themselves in opposition to a world that was considered to be undeveloped or pre-modern and in that sense primitive? Similarly, the new nation of the United States of America regarded the religious conflicts of Europe as primitive and barbaric; theirs was to be a secular society in which religion could flourish without being the source of vindictive and murderous conflict. Ancient Israel also typified its own neighbors as animals, and pigs or monkeys have been used in various countries to typify those who, being aboriginal or uncouth, have seemed primitive by a society's own moral or aesthetic standards. Societies typically tend to see those outside not only their territorial but their own normative borders as primitive: it is the tribe in the hills or in the other valley whose rites for the departed seem bizarre.

Even without these conventional forms of symbolic opposition, however, the world outside a society's knowledge and control is not only unknown but also can be mysterious and even frightening. It is in the bush outside the village or at night that spirits and demons prevail, and one is more likely to meet ghosts in such places, at crossroads or in ravines, at dusk or just before dawn, than in the broad light of day or in the boardroom. It is in such marginal places after all that one needs tokens of the sacred to fend off evil influences, and crosses at crossroads provide a sympathetic form of magic to keep the dead away. Indeed, the sacred is a way of defeating the primitive aspects of social life and of the psyche by imitating them.[2] Idols are, after all, images of the spirits they seek to evoke and yet propitiate and fend off.

The sacred emerges wherever a sign is placed to resemble and yet to fend off the unknown, the mysterious and the frightening. The cairn on a mountain top, like the cross along the highway where someone died in an automobile accident, is a reminder of the dead and yet also a prophylactic of sorts. Like cemeteries and shrines, these monuments and symbols are markers of places where one may remember the dead without encountering them. Where the unknown meets the familiar, there is always something uncanny, and it is the work of the sacred to domesticate the strange just enough to make it seem accessible but not really dangerous. Like the Maginot Line in 1914 along the border between France and Germany as a defense against German tanks, the sacred can be the object of a great deal of misplaced faith.

The shape of the sacred thus depends on what aspects of the psyche and of the environment seem to be beyond the pale of the human and the social, that is, the primitive. Whatever is anti-social or sub-human, and whatever subverts the reign of convention, or whatever defies notions of reason, represents the primitive. Indeed, the primitive represents the range of possibilities that is excluded from any society or social system. That is why hell, as we shall see in this book, is so often populated by those who are partly bestial, or crooked and corrupting.

Because it is the reservoir of excluded possibility, the primitive may at times seem to be the source of lost insights, virtues and vitality. In the Reformation, as scholastic understandings of theology became far more abstruse and complex than could be grasped by the laity, some demanded a return to the simple, the basic and the original. Individuals were to be allowed access to Holy Scripture on their own terms. Similar attacks were made on the unnecessary complexities of church life and organization. The order of religious institutions should resemble as far as possible the aboriginal simplicity of the early church, and religious speech should be plain rather than burdened with scholarship. In the same fashion, moreover, and often aided by the Reformation, scientific inquiry also sought to get down to the basics and to origins in a Table of Elements and in the fundamental laws of nature. To penetrate the mysteries either of the faith or of the universe, it was necessary to encounter the primitive on its own terms.

Indeed, the recent completion of a map of the human genome is an outcome of these earlier attempts to get back to the simplicity of origins, and it is no accident that the effort has focussed on the most primitive of all forms of life, the gene itself. In that effort, furthermore, humans are discovering that they share literally thousands of genes with the worm and the fruit fly, as science redraws the boundaries between the developed and the primitive. The study of chimpanzees, for instance, has shed light on the origins of the human understanding of obligation, reconciliation, justice and providence, and, as we shall see in this book, requires us to re-think the nature of the human psyche.

If there is a final boundary to be crossed on the way to recovering a sense of the primitive, I will argue, it is in the understanding of the psyche and particularly of the unconscious. That boundary, however, is guarded by representatives of the sacred: by images of subterranean worlds where strange and destructive passions continue to outlive their usefulness. In psychoanalytic terms the sacred is thus a massive defense against the inner world of the psyche that entices and threatens us but nevertheless eludes our knowledge and control. Thus we people the world with passions that we ascribe to animals and call them bestial, and we attribute to ourselves 'animal spirits' that we imagine to be more playful and vigorously creative than the destructive passions of mere beasts. In the sacred these passions take on the image of kings who are 'lion-hearted' or of gods that have wings or the head of a jackal. As in dreams, so in the sacred, these symbols both represent and disguise the passions themselves. The dream allows us to recognize ourselves in these disguises, these masks, even when we can also distance ourselves from them and say that these figures are sacred. We call them idols: *eidola*.[3]

Moreover, the dream, as the expression of the unconscious, has been an underground stream from which have emerged many of the images that have shaped the imagination and defined the longings and aspirations of Christians over many centuries. Not all the dreams have been claimed by religious thinkers; Constantine's own dream of being led to victory under the sign of the cross has had political and religious consequences for a millennium and a half. It is not stretching a point to say that Western societies have been living or acting out this dream as they sought to pacify first the Saxons and later the peoples of the 'New World.' If there is to be a renewal of Christian thinking and aspiration in our time, I would argue, it will have to come from a rediscovery of the dream: not only in the metaphorical sense of a vision, perhaps of racial equality, but in the quite literal sense of the individual's own reservoir of suppressed and unconscious memories and yearnings, magical thinking and wounded or grandiose self-imagery. That is why I am writing this book.

## Notes

1   Martha Himmelfarb (1983), *Tours of Hell. An Apocalyptic Form in Jewish and Christian Literature*, Philadelphia: The University of Pennsylvania Press.
2   I have developed this theory in several places; see especially *Beyond Idols*, Oxford University Press, 2001.
3   Patricia Cox Miller (1994), *Dreams in Late Antiquity. Studies in the Imagination of a Culture*, Princeton NJ: Princeton University Press, p. 49.

# Chapter 1

# The Social Construction of the Primitive

No society, of course, can include within itself all the ways of being human; otherwise it would have no boundaries, normative or territorial. Every society must therefore decide what is beyond the range of legitimate exploration, discovery, achievement, relationship and satisfaction. Possibilities that are excluded are then typified as indecent or uncivilized, sub-human or superhuman, bestial or angelic. Indeed, Satan was a fallen angel, and is often bestial or sub-human and inclined to make indecent propositions to the civilized.

However, this reference to Satan suggests that one of the functions of religion in the past has been to embody the knowledge of possibilities that would otherwise seem to be excluded. 'Seem' is the operative word in the last sentence, since Satan, for instance, is always likely to return and to suggest that some possibilities that were considered foreclosed or beyond the imagination are really quite practicable. That is the burden of the message of the serpent in the myth of the Garden of Eden, who asks whether God did indeed exclude the possibility of certain kinds of knowledge. Suddenly the unimaginable becomes thinkable or even possible. That is the function of religious language, and it is particularly obvious in religious speech about time. If the excluded possibility is relegated to a distant past or future, religious prophecy, for instance, may announce the day when the ancestors will return: the past and the future becoming embodied as well as foreshadowed in the act of religious speech itself.

However, the line between the sacred and the mundane or profane usually reinforces the normative boundaries of societies and separates the conceivable from the inconceivable, the knowable from the impenetrably mysterious, the possible from the impossible, and the uncertain from the likely. Thus shrines and saints, creeds and doctrines mark the boundary between the truly human and the sub-human or animal, between the social and the merely natural.

What I will call the Sacred (capital S) is inevitably subversive, because it represents a conception of time that is not wholly amenable to abstraction and irreversibility. The Sacred is thus the excluded possibility: indefinite, elusive, evanescent, undetermined, and yet potentially immediate, constraining, revelatory, disruptive. Wherever the Sacred is brought under the auspices of religion, possibilities that had been put beyond the pale of

5

experience are rediscovered. Take, for example, a carnival where people are allowed a brief flirtation with sexuality or a temporary release from the obligations of domesticity and slavery. Indeed such exploration may extend to the boundaries of the natural, the human, and of life itself. The question is whether religion in modern societies can still embody the Sacred or whether in fact religion has already lost its ability to incorporate the immediate and the distant, the mysterious and the conceivable, the impossible and the practicable in liturgy or in everyday life.

The sacred (the institutionalized Sacred) consists of a fragile set of symbolic defenses that mimics the entire range of possibility with a substitute and counterfeit pantheon of possibilities. It offers a form of service that claims to be perfect freedom, and a form of renunciation that promises to give to the faithful the consummation of every desire. Thus the sacred is a way of finding a safe place and time for the special graces, the charisma, of intimate, intense and enduring but evanescent and distant relationships.

Other possibilities that are not thus sanctified or made legitimate remain in the shadowy realm of the primitive: an earthy, but therefore both vital and possibly deadly source of energy and desire. These excluded possibilities, however, represent more than an external threat to the social order. Because they are contained within every psyche, at least in the unconscious, they represent a subversive 'fifth column' of possibility. Societies are thus betrayed from within and from below, by the unconscious. Those who are only partially socialized into the workings of the social system are still bearers of illegitimate aspiration and desire, and they are all the more likely therefore to give the lie to the sacred and to disclose its origins in the primitive. That is why it is the retrograde and the unregenerate who so often have been imagined to be the primary residents of hell. Kings and princes, as we shall see, are later additions.[1]

Of course, every society seeks to be emblematic of humanity at its best. Outside its moral or geographic boundaries lie other ways of being human, but these must be excluded successfully or otherwise discredited as being underdeveloped, uncivilized, or even sub-human and bestial. These excluded possibilities may be thought to carry an elemental life force whether they are seen as angelic or animal spirits. A particularly intriguing example, which we will discuss in more detail later in this book, is Freud's celebrated argument in *Moses and Monotheism* that Christianity reintroduced primitive elements that had long been repressed, sublimated, or otherwise excluded from Jewish religion.[2] He had in mind particularly the rebellion of the brothers against the autocratic rule of the father, but he associated that rebellion with such other signs of the primitive as the rule of women and the recovery of magical thinking. For Freud, of course, Jewish religion had long achieved heights that put it at a considerable remove from such vestiges of the primitive horde.

Clearly on the mind of Freud at the time, writing as he was in the late 1930s, were the primitive passions then fueling the politics and policies of the German State under Nazism. For Freud the worship of the Führer was another sign of the return of the primitive desire of the rebellious fraternity to re-instate the authority of the displaced father. Rebellion and revolution thus become the prelude to new tyrannies of a more democratic and egalitarian sort: hostile to superiority of any kind, and suspicious of all authority other than that of the self-imposed rule of the brothers themselves. Patriarchy thus returns with a vengeance under the guise of fraternity. I bring this up now to suggest how difficult it is in modern societies to draw the line between the primitive and the civilized, the animal and the human. That is why Nazism has been variously explained as a regression to a tribal past and as the height of a rationalized and technological society.

For Freud, of course, the primitive horde of rebellious brothers was to be found in the pre-history of Israel among the Ammonite priesthood that long had resisted the patriarchal tradition, carried by the Aaronite priesthood and initiated by Moses himself. The cultural contest had long been one between the heirs of Ikhnaton and his high, monotheistic theology and the competitive, tribal gods of the people surrounding the Hebrews in the Near East of whom Yahweh was one of the more competitive and successful. These latter possibilities, excluded in the long run by the return of Israel to the Mosaic/Egyptian tradition, were the primitive incarnate.

The primitive, however, is not what it used to be. For instance, I find it difficult to accept Freud's distinction between the superiority of a highly intellectualized and ethical system, such as Israel's, and the primitive, rebellious horde of the Near Eastern peoples. That is in part because what Freud thought of as a highly evolved and superior religion can also, like that of a rebellious male fraternity, be found to have had evolutionary predecessors among primates. From a first glance at the behavior of chimpanzees, for instance, it might seem that Freud was quite right about the primitive tendency of young males to resent the dominant male's monopoly on females and to do whatever they can to overthrow his oppressive limitations on their behavior, rights and satisfactions.[3] They will take what liberties they can, and they are far more likely to take risks when they believe that the dominant male is either not watching or cannot see them. However, they display all the appropriate signs of submission or – as humans would put it – of guilt when, after a mating spree, they find that the dominant male has returned. Lowered tails, averted glances and nervous grins are just the outward and more readily visible signs of an eagerness to appease what they have every reason to expect would be a wrathful ruler. It may well be, then, that the fear of the dominant primate was the beginning of a much later and more human wisdom about excluding certain possibilities from the range of legitimate expectation as being too primitive. Moreover, boys themselves become more hierarchical when they have to face external enemies; the father-principle returns when there is competition or danger at hand.[4]

Infractions of higher authority among some primates, moreover, are often dealt with in ways that seem relatively humane when compared with the behavior of other primates: rhesus monkeys having a lot to learn, for instance, from the chimpanzees. Dominant males are capable of making allowances as well as administering punishment. They may restore the disobedient as well as re-assert their own authority, and they may provide protection as well as insist on compliance and respect. Indeed, there seems to be something of a rudimentary covenant '... in which the lower echelons back the reigning powers, provided these guarantee their security.'[5] The rudiments of covenants, of moral systems binding the ruler to the ruled, can be found among the primitive primates.

Thus, argues De Waals, '... rule-learning, rule-testing, internalization, and guiltlike behavior are observable in our closest relatives,' the chimpanzee, although it has been left to humans to refine their belief '... in the watchful eye of an omnipresent God, in retribution after death, and in a connection between moral decay and natural catastrophes.'[6] Freud may have been right that the Jewish people possessed a highly developed religion, one that relied on a transcendent deity whose justice, like his thoughts, were not like those of mere mortals, and whose requirements were uniform and profound. In the light of De Waals's research on the way in which certain primates maintain order among themselves and cope with various forms of disturbance and disobedience, however, it would seem that such an achievement still betrays its own origin in the primitive, just as the primitive was in turn a by-product of conceptions of what is truly social, human and exalted.

If the primitive is returning in modern societies, then, it is not simply because certain kinds of behavior seem to be more prevalent. It is in part because it is harder than ever to draw the line between the human and the animal, the civilized and the primitive itself. For instance, De Waals goes on to point out that chimpanzees are unique in various ways, especially the extent to which they co-ordinate their actions during a hunt and, after a kill, make sure that everyone in the community has food.[7] They are also unusual in the way that the dominant males intervene to restore order in their communities or share food even when they are not having anything to eat themselves. Not only do they show high levels of impartiality even when their own relatives and allies are involved, but they also tend to side with those who are at a disadvantage.[8] They display an option, so to speak, for the poor and the oppressed.

Thus the construction of civilization and of notions of a high God relegated to the primitive what was in fact the source of higher impulses toward community obligation, sharing, duty and obedience. That is why, when Freud did find something primitive in Israelite religion and especially in the Mosaic code, it was the law of an eye for an eye, the *lex talionis*. On this point, he is more than upheld by these studies of the chimpanzee. As De Waals notes, there is a strong sense of reciprocity among the chimpanzees: those who do not share their food will not be helped in hard times, and those who fail to reciprocate are indeed the object of what from a human perspective looks remarkably like moral indignation.[9] As St. Paul put it, those who do not work will not eat (Thess. 3:10). There is another side to reciprocity, of course: revenge. Among chimpanzees, those who hold power may expect challenges from those whom they have successfully dominated in the past. Thus, De Waals concludes that '... the actions of our ancestors were guided by gratitude, obligation, retribution, and indignation long before they developed enough language capacity for moral discourse.'[10]

To summarize: societies lose their own bearings and deprive themselves of vital sources of both energy and virtue when they eliminate certain possibilities as primitive. However, they need to do so precisely in order to be social systems: a system being by definition one that excludes certain possibilities that are thereby relegated to the social and natural environment. In this book I will be arguing the case that it has been the function of religious language to embody and explore these excluded possibilities. That is why religious language speaks of transcendence and the infinite range of possibility attributed to the divine. I will illustrate this capacity of language from aspects of the Western Christian tradition that have explored the imagination and particularly the unconscious through the interpretation of dreams: the unconscious being perhaps the one frontier that has remained relatively continuous over time and that remains relatively resistant to social control.

Further, I will argue that a descent into the environment, so to speak, of the unconscious has been essential to the vitality not only of societies but of individuals. However, to both societies and individuals the unconscious remains primitive and therefore threatening. It is no wonder that societies construe the primitive in various ways that make it seem strange, inaccessible and dangerous. Certainly it is difficult for individuals to undertake an exploration of that forbidden territory under their own guidance. I will suggest that just such an exploration into the primitive is necessary, however, if individuals are to relinquish parts of themselves that have been slow to mature or to recover parts of themselves that have long been lost because they are too painful or embarrassing to recollect or to incorporate into a person's sense of self.

We are thus engaging four questions in this book: How do societies identify themselves by constructing a world of the 'primitive'? How do individuals experience, engage and explore the primitive, especially as a dimension of their own psyches? How does religious language both embody and disguise the primitive? And how does the psychoanalytic tradition incorporate and transcend the function of religious language in expressing and understanding the primitive?

If among humans the sense of obligation and gratitude has become refined and obscured, it is because of the capacity of language to elaborate endlessly such primitive knowledge until it requires the assistance of an expert to make matters plain. The primitive, the intuitively understood, the unconscious sense of guilt for nameless or imaginary crimes, the sense of a primordial debt that has yet to be paid, and the feeling that one is being watched by a powerful and omniscient being whose presence may prove either necessary or disastrous: all these are legacies from the world of the primate. The more they have received exquisite elaboration from priests, prophets and religious intellectuals, the more individuals have lost the capacity to decide for themselves what possibilities remain beyond the pale of legitimate expectation and what may be seized.

To explore for oneself a wide range of excluded possibility is to undertake a spiritual journey. That journey may lead outward from the center of civilization to remote places and even to the desert. It may also lead inward to the realm of the unconscious. For some that journey has led to both places: to the desert and to the world of fantasies and dreams. Certainly, for hundreds of years before and after the turn of the Christian Era, the journey to the world of excluded possibility has taken the form of what Martha Himmelfarb has aptly terms 'tours of hell.'[11] These tours witness people who are apparently receiving 'an eye for an eye': the just punishment for their sins and crimes. Such journeys, Himmelfarb argues, can be found in a wide range of Jewish as well as Greek and, later, Christian documents, and they owe much to their own Mediterranean and Egyptian sources.[12] We will therefore explore some of the attempts by Christian ascetics and visionaries to understand the unconscious through the metaphor of a descent into hell and the interpretation of dreams. We will also explore the role of literary and romantic language, in envisaging the realm of the unconscious and in exploring hell itself. In each case I will be investigating the ways in which the psychoanalytic tradition can incorporate, complete and correct particular aspects of these religious and literary excursions into the unconscious.

It is in the realm of the unconscious, of course, that primitive yearnings return to haunt the human imagination. There old rivals return to exact revenge for crimes that we have committed against them, if only in our fantasies. There also can be found the eye of the absent authority who knows our every move and remembers our infractions against his will. There, too, can be found memories of primitive sharing and of needs being met without a word having been uttered: a primordial world of silent communion and implicit understanding. As we now know, we are not the only ones who grieve; so do other primates who have lost their mothers. If we are to recover the soul, the *anima,* then, it will be necessary to recover what unites us to our animal legacy. On this point, Freud argued, we must infer that humans have an unconscious that bears the residues of a time before history. To descend into the realm of grief and of ancient passions is therefore to undertake a journey into the unconscious that links us once again with the primitive, pre-human past. No longer is it therefore so easy for any theoretical framework, religious or anthropological or psychoanalytic, to exclude certain possibilities as being merely bestial or supernatural: not truly human.

Certainly religion no longer has a monopoly on the authority to assign some possibilities to the world of the unknown and mysterious and others to the world of reasonable imagination and expectation. More to the point, I would argue that many of the Christian churches have lost the capacity to translate the possibilities that inhere in the soul into language that makes those possibilities accessible to the ordinary imagination. That is perhaps why so many denominations no longer speak a language that reveals individuals to themselves and challenges their self-understanding.

More than churches are endangered by this loss of imaginative language. Any society that lacks a capacity to understand the language of the soul will be at a loss for words to encompass the possibilities that reside in the depths of the psyche. Such a society will not understand the world that Freud explored, in which the differences among dreams, delusions and normal states of mind are difficult to determine. Such a society may reside under the illusion that the strange and the uncanny are social states reserved for primitive societies or for occult religious experience, but it will do so at the expense of losing vital sources of imagination, energy, and of virtue.

In losing the language of the soul, furthermore, religious institutions and whole societies lose a major source of their own capacity to evoke loyalty and commitment, to stimulate the social imagination, and to undergo the risks and uncertainty of radical social change. That is because the really primitive, the original source of threat and of promise, undermines any image of itself. This is true whether the sacred contains images of God, of beatified brothers and sisters, and of parents who have been turned into honored (and feared) ancestors, or whether it consists of mental images of the sub-human and the bestial, of enemies and rivals who are more like animals than people. The range of identification, loyalty and affiliation becomes far wider and thus also more problematical, the more the language of the unconscious is made articulate. So does the range of permissible affection and aggression.

The knowledge of mortality and of illicit desire returns with the language of the unconscious: the prohibited knowledge of good and evil. At times, certain possibilities for self-understanding or for expanding a society's network of loyalty and affiliation will therefore seem to be inherently life-giving, but the same possibilities may also seem to be on the side of death rather than of life, because they will bear the stigmata of evil. The unconscious reveals the clay feet of the idol that it also created, and those feet, like Satan's, may also be cloven. No wonder that the serpent in the myth of Eden suggests that there are other possibilities than the ones that God has endorsed. Religious language, when it is adequate to the task, can indeed incorporate possibilities that to a person or to a society may seem too illicit or dangerous to contemplate.

It is therefore not surprising that the very sources of religious imagination create imagery and a language that are full of internal contradiction. Images of a Virgin Mother reveal on her lap the source of that imagery: a young boy who commands the insignia of world domination and who rules in the absence of a father. The gargoyle on the corner of a cathedral roof not only provides an image of bestial passion but also reveals the animal spirits that fed the imagination of the Church and have fueled the ambitions of the builders. These, once again, are the clay feet that betray the origins of the religious imagination in the unconscious and in the legacy of the pre-human past.

Societies construe as primitive that which is beyond the borders of their knowledge and imagination. Like the prohibited fruit in the Garden of Eden myth, the primitive in the form of the unconscious is mysterious and potentially threatening, yet also full of vitality. At least, that is what I hope to show by focussing briefly on the dreams and fantasies of Christian ascetics and visionaries, whose thoughts lie somewhere between waking and dreaming. Thus the primitive in general, and the unconscious in particular, is thought to be the realm of the Sacred.

However, the primitive is also that which exceeds the realm of common decency; primitives, as I have noted, are likened to the native: aboriginal and therefore close to nature and the beginnings of humanity, but also uncivilized or even barbaric in their customs. That is why people thought to be primitive have felt their own worth and dignity to be undermined by those who have been able to stand on ceremony and who have had access to whatever graces and advantages a society can provide. It is usually the natives who have not forgotten the dreams of ancient glory that the more civilized have sublimated into symbol and architecture, into ritual and doctrine. That is why primitives are dangerous as keepers of the secrets of a more perverse religious imagination. They represent possibilities and passions that the more civilized claim to have excluded. No wonder that 'primitives' may seem a bit barbaric, unpredictable, unsociable, uncouth, a touch on the wild side. Like Marx's proletariat, the primitives are an essential source of raw energy, of strength and vitality, of productivity and the drive to consume.

For the same reason, however, those who are thought to be 'primitive' can be a major force for secularizing the sacred. Primitives are iconoclasts where idols are concerned; their very presence reveals the reality behind and underneath the image in the dream or in the sanctuary. The unconscious urge to triumph over rivals underlies religious images of victory over infidels and apostates, just as unconscious erotic attachment may feed an ascetic's visions of a loved one transfigured by divine light. Here the point is simply that religious language can embody not only what a society takes to be sacred but can include images of possibilities that have been excluded precisely because they may undermine the sacred. The myth of the Garden of Eden includes not only the tree of prohibited knowledge but the serpent who suggests other possibilities.

A gender or a race, a species or a group of people whose passions are somewhere between the civilized and the primitive are far from a modern invention. Take, for example, Jan Bremmer's study of the soul in ancient Greece, in which he has noted legends of a return of certain kinds of people, sometimes called 'Kares,' at other times 'Keres,' at certain festival occasions. These mythic people lived 'at the margin of Athenian society' but returned, during a festival called the 'Anthesteria,' to occupy for a brief moment a prominent position in the festivities.[13] Bremmer goes on to compare them to the masked invaders, or to the elves and witches, who have been legendary participants in comparable festivals in various European communities, even into the twentieth century.[14] They are perennial, dangerous, vital, and they represent not only a source of images of the sacred and demonic but also a threat to every form of the sacred. Even when formal religious language becomes emptied of its contradictions, the contrary forces of the sacred and the primitive may still be found in popular festivals.

I have been suggesting that every society excludes certain possibilities, and with them certain people, who are suffered, at best, in roles that are marginal and who bring pollution with them because of their association with what lies outside the borders of the system. In that marginal territory, those who represent the excluded possibility may become the objects of attraction as well as of fear, and they represent the possible return of the primitive whether in the form of redemption or vengeance. Thus those who come into the city at the time of a festival like the Anthesteria 'are all representatives of a demonic, non-social, unstructured world who are absent in normal times,' and they may often be associated with enemy soldiers or supernatural beings who bring the possibility of rebellion or revolution to the otherwise calm precincts of the city.[15]

Thus every society has a way of characterizing as primitive those who do not speak the language of the more cultivated. Usually the so-called primitives are thought to have less control over their aggressive and sexual drives and therefore seem to embody a threat to those who enjoy privileged access to sources of authority and satisfaction. Early resistance to psychoanalytic insight, for instance, may have stemmed from fear of infantile sexuality and childish dreams of glory. Children are always seen as both primitive and as yet carrying the future of the community or society in their souls.

The more complex and rationalized a society becomes, the more open it is to a wide range of possibilities. Modern societies are therefore especially likely to be host to alien presences, whether gods and angels, spirits or demons, the living and the dead, the animal or the anima. They will also be more open to previously excluded possibilities of selfhood: to the unsocialized aspects of the self, the inner self, the soul, that are resistant to any appeals to be civilized or even merely realistic. Even in these relatively more open societies, however, 'primitives' embody the very possibilities that these societies' values and standards claim to have excluded: uncivil ambitions to dominate and exploit others, or licentious and brutal pleasures.

In much the same way every society seeks to make invidious distinctions such as those that separate women from men: women being relegated to a sub-category of man with passions that are allegedly greedier, earthier, and inevitably therefore more difficult to satisfy and more dangerous to social order. That is why women so frequently do the work of tending to the body of the sick, of preparing bodies for burial, of grieving for the dead and dying, and of tending the grave. Women are thus ideologically relegated to what is inherently more primitive and natural as opposed to what is intrinsically social and humane or socialized. It is the natural aspects of the self, after all, that are thought to be a perennial danger to the social, a source of vital but dangerous energies and desire or of fatal propensities. The beautiful but dangerous women who work for the evil and destructive genius in James Bond movies are a case in point. As in these same movies, these women bear a disproportionate share of the blame for evil and of the costs of maintaining civilization, although the primitive passions of some of them can in the end be turned to good.

It is therefore not surprising that so-called 'primitives' become tired of listening to communications that they cannot understand, of being left out of the loop of gossip and decision making, of being regarded as local or provincial, of being told that their place is in the home or in the ethnic community where they have been forced to reside because they cannot afford the alternative. They resent being relegated to the status of the retired, the superfluous and the unwanted. They dislike being referred to as 'you people' or of being belittled by secular humanists, scolded by social workers, beaten by cops, condescended to by the clergy, studied by sociologists, and ignored on the street by those who have important places to go and significant people to see.

To underestimate what this sort of treatment can do to the soul is to miss the extent of untold agony in any society. Take, for example, the experience of growing up as a girl and later as a young woman while knowing all the time that one's very being, one's life, one's innermost self was not to be so highly valued as that of a man. No matter how appreciated a daughter might be as, for example, the apple of her father's eye, she may nonetheless be aware that she simply does not matter as much as her brother who is being prepared for important roles or who is being blessed with the patrimony of the father's spiritual authority. Why should such women not therefore abandon the shrines, ceremonies and customs of what has systematically demeaned them? Why not pour contempt on a society's pride?

The point is that those who embody the possibilities excluded by any social system are going to suffer, and they suffer very badly indeed. If the women's movement has tried to convey anything, beyond a sense of outrage and injustice, it is that to be the excluded possibility hurts deeply. Often this suffering is communicated with grace at a fairly high level of abstraction. Take, for example, this rather gentle but pointed comment by Linda Woodhead, a theologian and ethicist widely read in sociology and anthropology. Speaking of the work of Stanley Hauerwas, she points out that he relies largely on metaphors and allusions that exclude women: bricklaying, baseball, cricket and the like. As Woodhead puts it, 'Whilst not wholly incomprehensible, these are the sorts of metaphors which induce in women a common sense of standing under signs to which they do not belong.'[16] These signs mock women, much as the sign on the cross, 'King of the Jews,' mocked Jesus with a reminder of the very possibility from which he was being excluded in the crucifixion.

It is nothing new to suggest that metaphors and signs point to the very possibilities that are excluded. Language reminds us of what is placed beyond the pale of realistic or decent expectation in any society. Religious language, however, does more than point to the excluded possibility; it embodies it in the very act of speaking. That is indeed what invocation means and why certain things cannot be uttered 'in vain.' Religious language, then, is a double-edged sword, so to speak. It creates the domain of the possible by cutting off what is beyond the realm of the possible, but in doing so it also signifies and incorporates what is missing. That is what Christians have in mind, by the way, by the incarnate Word. It, too, is regarded as a two-edged sword that cuts both ways.

Woodhead goes on to point out the strategies by which theologians, for instance, manage to work without regard to the way that their own gender excludes certain possibilities in their thinking, their moral imagination and in their sensitivities. Some theologians are blinded by the invisibility of women in the theological academy and think that their own dominance is simply the way things are, normal and inevitable. They may suggest that no one is limited by gender from participating in the full range of possibilities that constitute any social order or even deny head-on that the use of masculine imagery and references in any way excludes the possibilities represented by women, their gender and their experience. To argue otherwise, they say, is to fall prey to outmoded 'Enlightenment' emphases on rights and self-realization.[17] Their language thus points to what it leaves out, but it fails to embody its own exclusions and loses the peculiar potency of religious language in its own abstractions.

Whenever a society makes distinctions, then, it differentiates, whether by segregating men from women, black from whites, or the old from the young. Those who live on the other side of the line of preferment know internally a judgement against their own being that has the effect of slowly eroding, and perhaps eventually killing, the soul. Those who embody the primitive, who represent the excluded possibility, all have received symbolic invitations to die, and to a soul unsure of its right to live, these invitations may be mortally wounding. It is understandable that the response of the 'primitive' occasionally has been murderous, and we have only seen the episodic signs of underlying rage.

Those who have been excluded from direct or even intimate association will increasingly come back to haunt those who have excluded them. Granted that those who have been marginalized are often regarded as primitive because they represent possibilities that have been excluded from more 'advanced' discourse or more highly developed institutions. Granted, furthermore, that these excluded possibilities may be represented by blackness or femininity, or even by the capacity to be in two places at the same time like ghosts or demons. That is perhaps why blacks in the United States used to be called spooks, just as women have been demonized as witches. In any form, however, they do come back to haunt those who occupy positions closer to the center of a society and whose discourse is thought to be more rather than less 'civilized.'

Either the primitive is acted out in a virtual reality where the imaginary and the actual are fused together at least during the liturgy itself, or the primitive is released on its own terms and is free to act out what has hitherto only been imagined. There is always the dangerous possibility that ancestors and the angels, the alien and the absent, the animal and the demonic do not always adhere to the prescribed time and place for their appearances. To maintain the primitive in its proper place requires that those who come into contact with it be set apart for that purpose. Only the ordained may carry out the symbolic act of breaking the taboo against violence, for example by breaking bread and pouring out wine. Others faithfully witness and condone the sacred action.

Where the primitive is tired of standing on ceremony, however, things do not go so smoothly. Performers trade places with witnesses. Buried hatred is dredged up. Actions are hardly stereotyped, and violence is no longer symbolic. In the crowds that seek to restore a primitive order, it is hard to distinguish the performers from the witnesses. Children go to schools with automatic weapons and military fatigues and eliminate those who have made fun of them. Even when some wear uniforms as the others watch people being marched off to be hung on trees or shipped out in cattle-trucks, they are clearly all engaged in acting out the primitive.

What of the in-between worlds, between rituals and crowds, between liturgies and vigilantes? Cannot the media mediate between these extremes? There are some who would argue that the primitive has more than enough outlets in the cinema, where the imaginary and the real are for the time being one and the same. In the movies, however, nothing is done once and for all. The same show plays again and again, but no one is really married or sentenced or imprisoned or murdered or avenged or sanctified or released from further tribulation. There is no need for a dismissal at the end of the rite because nothing is done and nothing finished. That is why, when a media celebrity really does die a violent death, the shock of recognition and awakening is so sudden and brutal. No one was really surprised that Mother Teresa died, regardless of her obvious merits, but few imagined that Diana would die so soon, regardless of her actual and very evident taste for danger.

## Notes

1 Martha Himmelfarb (1983), *Tours of Hell. An Apocalyptic Form in Jewish and Christian Literature*, Philadelphia: The University of Pennsylvania Press, pp. 123–5.
2 Sigmund Freud, *Moses and Monotheism*, translated by Katherine Jones, 1939, New York: Vintage Books, p. 87.
3 In this discussion I am relying entirely on Frans de Waal (1996), *Good Natured. The Origins of Right and Wrong in Humans and Other Animals*, Cambridge, Mass., and London, UK: Harvard University Press.
4 Ibid., p. 103.
5 Ibid., p. 102.
6 Ibid., pp. 114–15.
7 Ibid., pp. 142–4.
8 Ibid., pp. 126–31.
9 Ibid., pp. 154–9.
10 Ibid., p. 161.
11 Himmelfarb, op. cit.
12 Himmelfarb, op. cit., Introduction, pp. 1–7.
13 Jan Bremmer, *The Early Greek Concept of the Soul*, Princeton, NJ: Princeton University Press, 1983, p. 117.
14 Ibid., pp. 115–20.
15 Ibid., pp. 117–18.
16 Linda Woodhead (2000), 'Can Women Love Stanley Hauerwas?', p. 167 (mimeographed essay).
17 Ibid., pp. 170–71.

# Chapter 2

# The Primitive Unconscious:
# The Dream as a Source of Sedition

The recovery of the depths of the psyche may therefore be difficult precisely because they tend to be excluded from the normal processes of communities and institutions. Certainly the intense, soulful speech of the religious enthusiast or of the poet is generally reserved for particular times and places and excluded from everyday conversation. Those who require special attention to their innermost selves are often housed in particular institutions designed for that purpose. Certainly many societies tend to be suspicious or even frightened of individuals who find within themselves their own sources of inspiration and authority.

The psyche provides a counterpoint to the demands of civilized social life whenever it makes its own demands for recognition, satisfaction and for sovereignty over its own passions. These may indeed be distracting and occasionally disruptive of work and the family. Certainly the demands of the psyche for recognition and authority may often be difficult to reconcile with the claims of the community or of the state, of work and politics, of friendship and the family. The soul is therefore perhaps the most widespread example of the possibility that is excluded from ordinary social life: the loss of the soul being understood, in David Martin's excellent formulation, as

> the dethronement and incarceration of that which should be sovereign, the erasure of essential markings, the averting of the face from the summit of being, the atomization of integrity, the deterioration in the realm of spirit of vital 'presence,' and a repulsive occupation by powers or turbulences making for destruction, darkness, and death.[1]

Those who dramatize the motions of the soul are therefore often regarded as primitive, and exercises designed to place the soul in the center of public attention are often regarded as tribal.

In small, cohesive societies, the soul of the individual is very likely to be suppressed and hidden; it is the individual, after all, who represents a threat to the social order of such highly demanding and stable communities. Those who think for themselves are a danger, since they represent the threat of a contrary focus for authority, allegiance and affection. That is why, as Bremmer points out, in ancient Greece, before the rise of the city of Athens and a more democratic society that relied on the will, commitment, and commonsense of the individual, the soul was often a poor shadow of the individual. Indeed, the soul was often merely a small animal like a mouse, or an actual shadow, or a bat that lacks a voice of its own and merely squeaks, or even a butterfly that merely flits rather than engages in purposeful movement.[2]

Take, for example, Jan Bremmer's account of an ancient Danish folk legend in which the soul of a young woman is personified in the form of a mouse.[3] In the tale a man with a spade notices a mouse seeking to ford a stream and lays down his spade to improvise a bridge for the animal. The mouse crosses the stream, pokes around under a large rock on the other side, and then returns once again over the spade to his home in a hillock of grass. No ordinary animal, the mouse possessed an uncanny beauty and was pure white. As the folktale goes on to explain, however, the mouse was the soul of a young woman asleep nearby who dreamed that she had crossed a strange bridge of wood and iron, and had found on the other side a 'grey stone castle' filled with treasures of silver and gold. Indeed, on waking, she and the man found the treasure together and 'were never poor again.'

Clearly as a personification of the soul of the young girl, the mouse was unsocialized and uncivil, indeed subhuman, but it was the key to the treasure buried in the heart of the young woman. Peter Brown, for instance, speaking of Chaucer's *House of Fame*, states that in 'the image of the lost and errant dreamer, there may be an allusion to the idea current in ancient literature and traditional tribal culture that, during sleep, the soul steps out of its bodily boundaries and wanders in other, no less real, worlds.'[4] It is no wonder that the soul, because it steps out of the prescribed social bounds, is regarded as primitive: unsocialized, uncivil, and perhaps dangerous.

To be sure, there were individuals of whose soul a solid image could be made, but they were legendary heroes, like Achilles. Only the extraordinary individual, the demigod, could be thought to possess a soul of his or her own, an *eidolon*.[5] The ordinary individual, weighed down under the pressures of a small community, could hardly be thought to possess an inward source of authority and autonomy like the soul.

The soul, then, is the possibility for selfhood that is more likely to be excluded in societies, the heavier is the burden of conformity on the individual. No one knows this better, of course, than the young, women, slaves, and those who are otherwise deprived of freedom of movement, like prisoners. It is their souls that are typically regarded as primitive, that is, undeveloped and subhuman. Let us return to the old Danish legend just described, in which a young girl personified in the form of a mouse, seeks a hidden treasure. If the treasure is indeed her soul, it is hidden, indeed weighed down, under a large grey rock: the symbol of onerous burden. The soul can only be found with the aid of a man, who offers his spade as a bridge. Thus something is diverted from its natural purpose and turned to an unnatural one for this feat of soul-recovery to be performed. Note that the spade is often associated with the (male) penetration of the (female) earth: a symbol for manhood and the male organ. Thus even in the dream the young girl is permitted to find her soul only by the aid of a masculine force that is beyond her ownership and control.

It will therefore not be surprising to find that in many Christian communities the psyche has been subjected to heavy scrutiny and placed under severe constraints. Certainly the monastic tradition has specialized in the discipline of the psyche. In the next chapter we will review a recent study of an early Christian ascetic, a monk who lived well into the fifth century CE, John Cassian. He took seriously the innermost thoughts and fantasies of the individual monk and devoted much of his study to the analysis and interpretation of dreams. Indeed, he was not atypical of the early Church. It is becoming increasingly clear that various strands of early Christian asceticism elevated the passions to something that has to be included in any notion of salvation. The passions are not merely to be transcended or ordered but transformed and fulfilled. They are essential to the fulfillment of the possibility of the new human being foreshadowed and made possible in the incarnation. That means that a descent into the depths of the passions will be absolutely necessary if the human being is to rise to the full heights made possible in the new dispensation, the dispensation of the second Adam.[6]

If one wanted to have his or her dreams taken seriously and to base spiritual claims on one's dream life, one had better be a king or a notable saint than an ordinary monastic. Paul Dutton puts it this way:

> Only God's elite received visions of true things and even then infrequently; most men and women dreamt common dreams only fit to be forgotten. Thus a linguistic distinction came to cloak a hierarchy of visionaries at the summit and mere dreamers at the bottom. In this way the divergent opinions of the Bible could be incorporated and a hierarchy of Christian power preserved. In fact, Gregory of Nyssa chose to recognize only two classes of dreams: the normal and the divinely prophetic. In the early Christian world the power of public dreaming fell to the Apostles and their saintly successors.[7]

Of course, there were exceptions. Later in this chapter we will briefly discuss a dream by quite an ordinary man, a very poor cleric in fourteenth-century England: a dream that was so seditious that it fed the enthusiasms of the Peasant Revolt of 1381.

Unauthorized accounts of dreams were especially suspect, and only those accounts that typically fit Biblical imagery and example were regarded with a minimum of suspicion. Fairly typical of the history of the Western church at least has been a rank suspicion of those who, whether Christian or not, claimed to have access to the mysteries of the soul. By the eighth century, Paul Dutton reminds us, '... the official line was that popular dream interpretation was a form of pagan divination.'[8] Those who claimed the spiritual authority to receive and interpret their own or others' dreams were regarded as beyond the pale of Christian civilization: pagan, in the sense of primitive in their practice of magic, casting spells and foretelling the future. Anything that 'smacked of divination' seemed to the Christian elite of the Carolingian empire to be a sad reminder of the very partial conversion of northern Europe and of the survival of pagan magical arts.[9]

Not all the dangerous sources of dreams and their interpretation, however, could be found in the pagan world outside the Church. Those who had the temerity to call their souls, and therefore their dreams, their own could also be found among the monastic orders and among laity who felt they had their own sources of divine inspiration. The danger, as Dutton so well puts it, was that 'Christ might still visit the faithful with corrective visions of penetrating truth.'[10] That is,

> At some profound level, dreams and visions promised or threatened, depending upon one's perspective, the uncertainties and intoxicating indeterminacies of continuing revelation: that somehow the divine story was not yet complete ...'[11]

As I noted in the first chapter, any society must exclude certain possibilities if it is to have social and physical, not to mention moral and intellectual, boundaries. Those possibilities that are excluded are the Sacred; in theological terms, they represent the possibility that God has as yet still more to reveal than is already known of ultimate possibility. Sociologically speaking, the Sacred is always therefore a threat to what a particular society or its major institutions like to hold sacred. No wonder, then, that the Church was very quick to call unofficial or private sources of dreams and their interpretation 'pagan.' The label itself suggests a realm of the Sacred that was beyond ecclesiastical knowledge and control and was therefore illicit, but nonetheless Sacred for being illegitimate. The official association of pagan and private divination with 'the demonic world of tree worship, spells, charms, love potions, and spirits' also reminds us that societies tend to construe alien possibilities as the 'primitive.'[12]

The alien and the primitive take up residence not only in the areas outside a society's boundaries but within as well. They inhabit the insufficiently compliant or the still somewhat unsocialized aspects of the psyche: the deeper, if not always wholly unconscious, reaches of the soul. That is why the clergy have inquired into the dreams of the laity for possible sources of dangerous as well as legitimate inspiration. In the sixteenth century, Catholic priests in Spain interrogated one young woman, Lucretia, who confided to her Catholic confessors several hundred dreams of a distinctly seditious nature, filled as they were with anti-monarchical ideas and sentiments.[13] However, priests in the sixteenth century were not the only ones able through the interpretation of dreams to inquire into the secrets of the soul. Holland notes that the analysis of dreams was a widespread activity 'trapped between the strong popular fascination with dreams, ably supported by the economics of the profession of oneiromancy, and the equally strong religious culture which wished their study to be placed within the bounds of the Church and hence the state.'[14] They were competitors in the race to conquer the mysteries of the psyche. Certainly these Catholic clerics were seeking to reduce the mystery that inheres in the psyche: possibilities for unauthorized revelation or for seditious fantasy. That is, to revert to the terms I was suggesting in the first chapter, the clergy in this case were seeking to reduce the Sacred to the sacred.

By capitalizing the Sacred I wish to allude to what is beyond the realm of religious belief and practice, beyond the scope of religious institutions and their agents. Rather it has been the role not of the clergy but of seers and shamans, mystics and prophets to point to otherwise unimaginable possibilities for social transformation or general disaster. To be sure, Christian doctrine points to such an area of mysterious possibility when it speaks of the second coming of Jesus Christ, but it cannot translate that mystery into prediction or precise anticipation without losing the force of its own religious imagination in the process. Similarly, Christian teaching concerning the death and resurrection of Christ continues to point to mystery only so long as the promises and possibilities of faith can never be fully imagined or elaborated, tested, and finally fulfilled or disappointed.

At its best, the Christian faith creates a reality principle that is open to the excluded possibilities in any social system. However, religious groups that divine the final consummation or explosion after a certain passage of time remove the Sacred from the area of mystery and place it in the domain of what I would call merely the 'sacred.' Institutionalized revelation thus partially removes the possible from the area of mystery and makes it known.

It has long been the function of the dream, and of those who seek to learn the language of the dream, to discern some of the possibilities that have been excluded not only from everyday life and from the normal workings of the heart and mind but from the authorized versions of sacred mystery. That is why exploring the hinterland of the dream world is like the experience of pilgrimage. As a pilgrim one leaves the familiar surroundings of work and home, of synagogue and church, abandons one's ordinary roles and social positions, and enters into a world into which the strange may yet become familiar. On the way, one may meet people who, although they are strangers, become familiar in the course of one's journey. Peter Brown, for instance, notes that 'acceptance of the state of being liminal, between heaven and hell, is a crucial movement toward spiritual enlightenment.'[15]

Thus, in revelation and through the dream, the Sacred becomes less mysterious; its secrets are revealed to the individual imagination. In the hands of the Church, as I have noted, the interpretation of dreams has long served to keep human aspirations within the limits of the sorts of satisfaction and authority that the Church was willing to grant to individuals. Now that other professions have acquired the authority to decipher the language of the unconscious and to regulate the interpretation of the dream, however, the limits of aspiration and personal authority have been expanded; no wonder that psychoanalysis has presented a threat to what Freud himself called the 'reality-principle': the agreed-upon limits on what individuals could claim for themselves.

What is at stake in the interpretation of the unconscious is the authority of the soul: an inner principle of vitality that disregarded the limits set by social authority and by life itself on what could be imagined, desired, sought for and claimed. That is why infants' sexuality seemed to Freud to be so 'polymorphous' and 'perverse'; it ranged over a variety of surfaces in search for possibilities that adults have longed learned to regard as beyond the pale of legitimate satisfaction. Perversity is simply the survival of that infantile disregard for the boundaries established by the larger society on what can be imagined and claimed for the individual's own purposes and satisfaction.

As Freud argued, however, whatever is excluded and repressed comes back in a disguised form not only in the dream but in the ordinary, everyday course of human events. Notably it is in ordinary language that the repressed elements make their appearance, disguised not only as slips of the tongue but as metaphors and similes, analogies and allusions that point to possible dangers or satisfactions that have been excluded from conventional expectation. Religious language is pre-eminently the place where one looks for these excluded possibilities: the sighs, as Marx put it, of the oppressed creature. That is, after all, what transcendence means: the set of possibilities that have been excluded from everyday life and are therefore supra-mundane.

As Freud himself argued, the Mosaic tradition is itself an example of the excluded possibility that returns, under the auspices of religious language, to the consciousness of a people and to a position of eventual domination. The people of Israel had once been in Egypt, long before they acquired what was later to become their official tradition, and, in their period of wandering and settlement in Israel, they had acquired a god, Yahweh, who, as Freud put it, resembled the surrounding Baalim. As their religion increasingly took on written form, the memories of Moses' Egyptian tradition were excluded from official record and consigned to folk memory, where they survived in an oral tradition that was plastic and yet faithful to its origins; thus

The Jewish people had abandoned the Aton religion which Moses had given them and had turned to the worship of another god who differed little from the Baalim of the neighboring tribes. All the efforts of later distorting influences failed to hide this humiliating fact. Yet the religion of Moses did not disappear without leaving a trace; a kind of memory of it had survived, a tradition perhaps obscured and distorted. It was this tradition of a great past that continued to work in the background, until it slowly gained more and more power over the mind of the people and at last succeeded in transforming the God Jahve into the Mosaic God and in waking to a new life the religion which Moses had instituted centuries before and which later had been forgotten. That a dormant tradition should exercise such a powerful influence on the spiritual life of a people is not a familiar conception.[16]

Here Freud clearly applies his notion of the return of the repressed to the history of religion in Israel. To do so he has to draw an analogy between the experiences of early childhood and those of the dawn of the people of Israel, and he focuses on the memory of a time that was seen as particularly enchanted because it had been filled with power and glory. It was a time like that of the latency period in childhood in which infantile dreams of glory have not been abandoned in favor of more realistic aspirations for later adult satisfactions. In latency, the fantasies of infancy thus acquire a longer life than reality normally permits and are therefore in a position to cause later disturbances when the present suffers in comparison with the imaginary past. At such times the individual, still under the magical spell of childhood, is like a people whose folk epic still enshrines a living memory of 'an obscure and incomplete tradition' of an 'eventful' and 'grandiose' period, 'the never forgotten dream of a Golden Age': the ancient Greeks with their Homeric tradition being a case in point.[17]

There is more here than a mere analogy between the legacies of childhood and those of an earlier, mythic period in the history of a people. In both cases we are witnessing the operation of two systems: one social, the other that of the psyche itself. In both cases there is an excluded possibility: the one a memory of ancient devotions to a high god, the other the memory of a magical world in which wishes seemed to come true and one had ineffable power over one's enemies. Both possibilities are 'excluded' because they do not serve the purposes of adapting either a people or a person to an environment that is hostile to its pretensions.

What is excluded thus becomes the 'environment.' That is, the possibilities for relationships between insiders and outsiders, possibilities for friendship, affection, affiliation, loyalty, subversion, treachery and outright warfare all are shaped by where each society (and each psyche) draws the line between what is part of the system and what is not. Conversely, what is excluded shapes the system. As with Russia under Stalin, the sense of being surrounded by a capitalist encirclement creates a defensive, even paranoid system eager to eradicate all capitalist influences from within. The sense of being surrounded by an alien people whose gods are dangerous, whether they be those of Egypt or later those of the neighbors of Israel in and around Palestine, dominates the internal politics of the nation and constrains friendship and affection within the limits of prescribed affiliation. What is outside the range of the system becomes unspeakable, unimaginable, mysterious, dangerous and always insidiously attractive.

What makes the fantasies of childhood, then, an appropriate analogy for the exclusion of Egyptian devotion by the early Israelites is their common fate: an element of the past that, as time passes, becomes a source of longing and embarrassment. It is a source of longing because the desires of infancy for immediate and eternal satisfaction, rapport and mastery are doomed to failure; they are placed in the past by the emerging ego of the child who recognizes that he or she will have to wait and, along the way, acquire the skills and authority appropriate to adulthood. They are a source of embarrassment because they leave a legacy of a sense of entitlement or of obligation that cannot be fulfilled in the present: entitlement, perhaps, to royal honors or obligation to pay an ancient debt. Similarly, the Israelites have long remembered that their ancestor (Moses) killed an Egyptian, just as they have long understood that they are a royal people destined someday to reign under the auspices of a high monotheism. Clearly Freud was disenchanted by these religious pretensions, just as he was aware that many of his patients were burdened either by a sense of princely entitlement because of their early sufferings or by guilt for crimes that they themselves had never committed. His patients, then, were like the Jews who needed to come to their adult senses after a long period of latency in which they had been entertaining hopeless dreams of glory and had nourished longstanding guilt and grievances.

Why, then, would I argue that religion should recover a sense of the excluded possibility? Is not the excluded possibility a legacy of an earlier, more primitive period in the life of the individual or of the nation that demands impossible satisfactions, claims undeserved rights, and aspires to dominate all rivals for affection and attention? To recall such a world of possibility could well inspire a new wave of religious conflicts or motivate a generation of believers to claim political authority that they have not earned in the marketplace of public opinion: witness Pat Buchanan's periodic calls for a revival of a Christian nation long suppressed by secular humanists and the Supreme Court. However, unless the latent antagonisms, dreams of glory and desires for revenge are allowed to come to the surface, they will operate more or less invisibly to make a people unnecessarily serious about their grandiose claims to a place of leadership among the nations of the world.

The primitive, as the cultural reservoir of such excluded possibilities, will always suggest possibilities for illicit satisfaction that, if achieved, could undermine the relationship between generations and genders or subvert all forms of domestic authority. Grandiosity, restlessness, distraction and subversion can be as self-defeating for a nation as they are for an individual. Therefore let the repressed elements of a nation's – or an individual's – unconscious return so that the impossible and the mysterious can be deprived of their uncanny and potent place in the imagination and exposed to discourse and the choice of an informed person or people. Let the rights of gays be discussed and voted upon. Let also the pretensions of a religious right be aired in the public arena of national debate. But also let the grievances of an African-American people still suffering from the effects not only of slavery but of generations of official and unofficial violence be brought to the attention of a nation where claims to recompense and reparation can be discussed and honored.

There is another reason why religious language should be able to discuss once again the ineffable, to imagine the unimaginable, and to think the unthinkable. What was once regarded as primitive and therefore to be transcended is now returning to demand attention and legitimacy. That is because the boundaries of complex societies like the United States are becoming increasingly permeable and vague. That is, it is no longer apparent what possibilities are excluded or should be excluded. Longings for the exchange of peoples, for immigration, for the relaxation of social codes of sexual legitimacy, for the admission of ancient guilt, for the satisfaction of long-standing grievances, and even for communication with those who are absent, unseen and perhaps non-existent: all these are expanding into the zone of the legitimate and the possible. If the religious imagination cannot find words with which to discuss these possibilities, the discussion will continue, as it has been going on, without the benefit of clergy.

Religious language possesses the capacity to embody possibilities excluded from social discourse and from the conventional imagination. Not merely to point to that possibility but to embody it: that is the core of religious speech. Thus the prophet ignores authorized channels and speaks in words that embody the excluded possibility; the prophet thus speaks 'a word from the Lord,' the word of God. Take, for example the long, late fourteenth-century poem, *Piers Plowman*.[18] Like the other visions that I will discuss in this book, and like Freud's own self-analysis, it uses the language of the dream to describe the passions and deceptions of the human soul. The author, William Langland, uses composite characters with names like Covetousness or Wrath to personify a range of motives, illusions and affections that stand outside the range of legitimate desire and aspiration. These dimensions of the psyche are also, no doubt, disguised forms of the author's own soul; he knows them well. No stranger to accusations of laziness or envy, to using the things of religion to some worldly advantage, the author is himself a cleric of the lower orders who relies on other people to give him and his wife enough food and clothing on which to live. He begs for a living in exchange for prayers, and in his dream-like vision he excoriates, among many others, clergy who scorn an honest day's work and use their office for gain. Again, the author seems to have known grief. He writes, as he says, because 'since my friends died I never found/A life that I liked except in these long robes.'[19] His poem, then, is in some ways a descent, like Dante's 'Inferno,' in *The Divine Comedy* into the land of grief.

I mention Langland's poem here because it suggests the way in which religious language can be used to explore what is beneath the surface of social life, beyond its moral boundaries, and outside the range of its imagination. Beneath the surface of social life, Langland's otherwise respectable characters steal, lie, fornicate, bribe, beat, corrupt, harass and ignore the poor and the unfortunate. These characters placate or deceive the kings, judges, bishops and priests who are supposed to provide truth and justice but who are themselves corrupted and who give pardons where there is no peace. Opposing the deception of every façade and of each soul is Truth, who will eventually prevail. It is not surprising that the Peasant's Revolt of 1381 drew some of its language and perhaps its inspiration from this poem.

What distinguishes this poem from an anarchist tract, say, of the nineteenth century is its understanding of the soul. Social life itself is nothing more than a theater that plays out and decides the fate of the soul. The ultimate fate of the soul depends on whether the truth is spoken, a bribe is given and received, a farmer's hayfield robbed, a case at court decided unfairly, or a spouse betrayed. All of social life is in fact a spiritual economy, and one should therefore, as Reason puts it, ' "get started on the life that is commendable and true to your soul." '[20]

This is not a recommendation that one find a job that allows one a measure of self-actualization, no matter how modern it sounds. It is a reminder that something infinitely and therefore immeasurably precious is at stake in the calculations of everyday life. Indeed, the words are addressed to the author himself by Reason in the course of the second dream of the poem. Earlier Langland's dreamer had been saying that he would rely on God to make up for his own losses, as if a special providence would come finally to his rescue. It is Reason, however, who reminds him that his spiritual fate should rely not on the chances of divine grace but on his own immediate decision to live a life 'commendable and true' to his soul.

Profoundly important as is the individual's responsibility for his or her own spiritual fate, for Langland it is also true that one's fate depends on the way one is treated by others. The society as a whole is a spiritual economy in which no one is saved who profits from or contributes to the spiritual deprivation of others. If priests accept money from usurers they will have to help the usurers repay that debt in purgatory. Thus there is a fine balance at work here: the calculations of the usurer on how much money can be gained over a certain amount of time are weighed in the balance of a spiritual debt that can only be repaid in the infinite time of purgatory itself. In that balance is weighed the incommensurable: profit, on the one hand, and the fate of the soul on the other.

Langland's poem thus discloses the depths and heights of what is at stake in the otherwise mundane or pragmatic exchanges of everyday life. If 'a whore can tithe better from what her ass earns her/Than can an errant usurer', so does a Bishop's fate at the last judgement depend on the sources of the money that he accepted during his lifetime; he will go down with the thieves if he has accepted their offerings.[21] Conversely, those who have 'had the poor for a wise-fool' at their tables, or who have cared in their lifetimes for 'a bed-ridden woman', or who have listened to the blind, will have comfort for their souls as they die and will avoid the pangs of purgatory and hell.[22] The meantime is the end time. That is why the calculation and management of possibility requires something more than political cajoling, punditry, or the abstract counsels of committees on ethics.

*Piers Plowman* brings to the surface what is normally concealed in everyday discourse. What ordinary conversation excludes finds embodiment in the poem's visionary language. Piers knows and speaks the Truth: ' "... whoever wants to learn where Truth lives,/I will show you right to his place." '[23] The poet then reveals the soul as suffering from the weight of unfair and crushing social practices, from the effects of official injustice and corruption, and from the vast indifference of the pious to human suffering and to the truth itself.[24]

Langland's prophetic poem lies outside the frame of ordinary language, is embodied in religious utterance, and uses the language of the unfettered soul. It belongs with the utterances of the Old Testament prophet which Peter Brown compares with Medieval English dream visions: both being forms of language released from the fetters of everyday life, conventional sociability and of authorized speech. For instance, with regard to Chaucer's *Book of the Duchess'* Brown argues that the soul's 'sense of relief, of vitality, and sociability after his denatured, alienated and claustrophobic waking existence is almost palpable.'[25] Religious language embodies formerly excluded possibility and is thus enabled to give a wake-up call, *Wachet Auf.*

Religious language, then, unless it is to die the death of a thousand qualifications, must carry and create the experience of the soul that has been awakened to new life. That is because religious language specializes in embodying the excluded possibility, and the soul, the depth of the psyche, is the most basic and important of those exclusions. Religious language embodies the revelation of the fettered and half-buried soul. For the speaker, the language is that of the dreamer who has come into the full possession, at last, of his or her subordinated faculties for sensation, experience, insight, understanding and authority. For instance, speaking of *Piers Plowman*, Brown notes that the dreamer-speaker 'sees things normally hidden, and the sense of having broken through to a fundamental level of understanding is very strong. The dream makes possible perceptions which, while anchored in the dreamer's spiritual self, are also moral, social, and political.'[26]

The revitalization of any religion depends in large part on its ability to recover what Fromm calls the forgotten language of the soul, and particularly of the unconscious. There one finds the hidden costs and the untold agony of any society, experienced at the deepest levels of the psyche. Unfortunately, the Church has long sought to master the language of the dream only in order to confine it to its quarters. Indeed, the controlling interest of the Church in the interpretation of dreams goes back at least as far as the seventh century to Pope Gregory the Great, who could attribute dreams to influences ranging from the contents of the stomach to divine inspirations.[27]

Although William Langland knew the instructions of Pope Gregory the Great, he preferred to disregard the ones that confine monks and nuns to their institutional quarters. For him the life of the city and the country was infinitely preferable to that of the monastery, even though it was far more strife-ridden and precarious. In the same way he opened up the interpretation of dreams to the possibility of a radical indictment of the social order and its crushing effects on the soul. He was a seeker after the truth of the mysteries that lay outside the moral order and beneath the conventional surfaces of the society. It was there that the costs of the system could be found, its dirty secrets and untold agony, and its possibilities for self-destruction and renewal.

The Truth is to be found, as Langland put it, in the experience of dreaming that continues to animate the individual and to haunt social life with the knowledge of undisclosed possibility. That is because the soul uses a language that points to and often embodies what it also excludes. Thus, as we will see, Freud could speak of the ghosts in his unconscious as the 'revenants,' the people and emotions that keep returning in one disguise or another. At other times, and often in the same context, he spoke of ghosts that kept returning as disguised aspects of himself, and so to understand them he had to speak of the feelings of loss or self-mortification that these ghosts in his psyche returned to represent. Like Langland's characters, Freud's were composed of himself and of others who stood for one or another unfortunate passion, like the Christian symbol of the cross. Notions such as a Second Coming or the final arrival of the Kingdom or the new era opened by the presence of the Holy Spirit, all these are assertions that the excluded possibility will not remain for ever beyond the precincts of the possible.

It is precisely this capacity of religious language, namely to speak of mystery in a way that breaks the veil separating the possible and the impossible, that has been lost in most religious communities. At least in the mainline Protestant denominations it is easier to speak of social issues or pastoral concerns than it is to use a language that evokes what it also veils and excludes. Perhaps the poverty of religious language is due not only to the professionalization of religious discourse but also to the near-monopoly of dream interpretation by therapists, psychiatrists and psychoanalysts. The result of this specialization of discourse is the Church's loss of social authority; it is no longer the prime inquisitor into thoughts that might prove dangerous to the state and redemptive to the soul.

## Notes

1 David Martin (1995), 'Bedeviled', Richard K. Fenn (ed.), in *On Losing the Soul: Essays in the Social Psychology of Religion*, Albany: State University of New York Press, p. 40.
2 Jan Bremmer (1983), *The Early Greek Concept of the Soul*, Princeton, NJ: Princeton University Press, pp. 66–9, 85.
3 Ibid., p. 117.
4 Peter Brown (1999), 'On the Borders of Middle English Dream Visions,' in Peter Brown (ed.), *Reading Dreams. The Interpretation of Dreams from Chaucer to Shakespeare*, Oxford: Oxford University Press, p. 29.
5 Jan Bremmer, op. cit., pp. 75, 78 ff.
6 Paul M. Blowers (1996), 'Gentiles of the Soul: Maximus the Confessor on the Substructure and Transformation of the Human Passions,' *Journal of Early Christian Studies*, **4**(1), 57–85.
7 Paul Dutton (1994), *The Politics of Dreaming in the Carolingian Empire*, Lincoln and London: University of Nebraska Press, p. 34.
8 Ibid., p. 38.
9 Ibid.
10 Ibid., p. 40.
11 Ibid.
12 Ibid.
13 Peter Holland (1999), 'The Interpretation of Dreams in the Renaissance,' in Peter Brown (ed.), *Reading Dreams. The Interpretation of Dreams from Chaucer to Shakespeare*, Oxford: Oxford University Press, pp. 139–40.
14 Ibid., p. 140.
15 Brown, op. cit., p. 48.
16 Sigmund Freud, *Moses and Monotheism*, translated by Katherine Jones, 1939, New York: Vintage Books, p. 87.
17 Ibid., pp. 87–9.
18 William Langland, *Piers Plowman, The C Version*, translated and with notes by George Economou (1996), Philadelphia: The University of Pennsylvania Press.
19 Ibid., Passus V, ll.40–41; p. 44.
20 Ibid., Passus V, ll.102–3; p. 46.
21 Ibid., Passus VI, ll.306–7, ll.340 ff.; pp. 57–8.
22 Ibid., Passus VII, ll.104–19; p. 64.
23 Ibid., Passus VII, ll.198–9; p. 66.
24 Ibid., Passus VII, ll.175–81; p. 66.
25 Brown, op. cit., p. 36.
26 Ibid.
27 Steven Kruger (1999), 'Medical and Moral Authority in the Late Medieval Dream,' in Peter Brown (ed.), pp. 59–60.

Chapter 3

# Searching for the Collective Unconscious: The Return of the Primitive Crime

Any society is a reservoir of old longings and ancient hatreds. These need to be understood, addressed, resolved and transcended if a society is to have a future that is different from its past. Furthermore, whatever a society tends to exclude as a set of possibilities may represent essential sources of energy or information, of neglected inspiration or authority. To face an enemy or to explore new territory may require animal spirits, just as a society may require a new openness to alien ways of thinking and living if it is to make use of ideas and technology developed by foreigners. Whenever a nation needs to resolve old hatreds and fulfill ancient aspirations while at the same time acquiring foreign ideas, capital and technology, it will need to open itself to a wide range of turbulent emotions and to face its own fears of alien influences. Under these conditions a society may develop an ideology that, like Japan's prior to the Second World War, seeks to use the modern to overcome modernity while mobilizing national sentiments around dreams of national glory and vindication. The fascist potential in such a situation is a matter of historical record as well as in the daily news.

The primitive thus returns whenever a society has to dig deeply into its own storehouse of memory and aspiration or when it needs to respond to a new set of opportunities and threats in its environment. To delve into the past, however, is to open up local, ethnic or national memories of past injuries and insults, and to envisage a new future is to promise long-delayed satisfaction. Thus the early Christian church thrived on anticipations of a new heaven and a new earth, but this radical departure also required that old hatreds be satisfied and old injuries avenged. There would be many who would therefore be cast into outer darkness with much gnashing of teeth among some quarters, while others, the beneficiaries of the new age, would enjoy the sight of their old rivals' anguish. The enemies of Satan would at last enjoy their triumph over both the gentile and Jewish enemies of the Church, who would suffer the pangs of damnation.

Under these conditions, I am arguing, the psyche is profoundly renewed. In order to take advantage of new opportunities and meet new threats, the psyche resolves old quarrels and anticipates a new future. To enter into these ancient animosities, however, and to rekindle old loves requires a descent into the depths of the psyche: a descent into a spiritual netherworld. The descent into hell, then, has been one way that religious traditions have imagined the recovery of the soul that has long been burdened with injustice, injury and the despair of hope far too long deferred. In this descent the pilgrim, like Dante, sees the consequences of old sins and the continuing effects of illicit, burning desire. In this descent the soul faces the full consequences of living in the past and learns, as did Dante, the futility of a pity for those for whom the future is only a continuation of the past and who thus have no time left at all. However, like current attempts to relive and dramatize the Holocaust in Nazi Germany, such a descent can indeed produce a renewal of determination that 'never again' would such a primitive passion overtake and consume a people now fully alert to the dangers immanent in the present or imminent in the future.

While such a descent may be necessary for the revitalization of a nation or the renewal of a religious tradition, it is also a dangerous journey from which some may not return. As I have noted, a people may develop an acquired taste for illicit and insatiable desires or a grim determination to avenge old injustices. Individuals, and especially those undertaking the descent into hell as an ascetic journey into the depths of the psyche, could either be permanently scarred by the journey or turn it into an interminable fascination with the underworld of the soul. In psychoanalytic terms, furthermore, a miscarried descent into the unconscious could lead to an interminable analysis.

Given the long duration of Christianity's fascination with the psychic underworld, it is an open question as to whether the Christian religion can be trusted in the future to provide guidance into those depths. For instance, could one expect the churches in the United States of America to open up painful memories of racial injustice in this country? Some churches would have to face more than the deep psychic wounds they have inflicted on African-Americans but also acknowledge the extraordinary religious impulses that fed slavery and lynching and that continue to feed racism in the religious right. It may well be that only a psychoanalytic approach can be expected to provide an exploration of the unconscious without offering an invitation to magical thinking or to grandiose fantasies of personal and national renewal and vindication.

There is a larger question hiding under this specific concern with whether or not Christianity is a reliable guide to the depths of the unconscious. Some writers credit Christianity with being a major force for secularization in the West. To be sure the Christian Church has been a major carrier of rationality in the West in part because of its investment in the co-ordination of complex organizations, policies and practices. Given its antagonism to competing or deviant sources of authority and inspiration, the Church has also been a major influence in the development of systematic theology, organizational control systems and professional discipline. Because of its commitment to a consistent pattern of belief and practice, the Church has long sought to eliminate anomalies and inconsistencies, especially when these enjoyed popular support or threatened the Church's monopoly on the means of salvation. Thus the Church has uprooted, co-opted or destroyed indigenous forms of piety and magic, and it has harbored a chronic suspicion of unauthorized religious enthusiasm. Add to these long-term influences the effect of a theology that lifts the divine far above the mundane and the transient. Such an abstract faith, however, still requires individuals to take personal responsibility for their belief and practice. The world becomes a place emptied of divine signposts and supports, while the individual is held responsible for charting his or her way through a maze of threats and opportunities. Under these conditions, religion no longer embodies the excluded possibilities of primitive desire and aspiration. When the primitive returns, therefore, it takes other shapes, like modern fascism.

Christianity is a major force for secularization, but it could yet again undertake the guidance of a person or a community, perhaps even of a people or of a nation, into the dangerous territory of the personal or collective psyche if, and I would argue only if, it can again articulate the psychic underworld of the individual and of the larger society. To once again encounter magical thinking without fostering it, to encourage a people to relive its old grievances without demanding satisfaction for them, and again to uncover ancient longings for harmony and communion without offering unrealistic prospects for their fulfillment, these would be the tasks of a Christianity whose language, like that of early medieval visionaries and of Dante himself, could embody the excluded possibilities of what once was understood to be the hell of the spiritual underworld. Individuals would continue to be held responsible for their encounters with the unconscious, even though the Church, like Virgil, would encourage them not to waste pity on those consumed by hopeless affections. Like Virgil, the Christian faith would provide reminders of the limits on human aspiration and mark the irreversible and inexorable passage of time, while at the same time pointing out what individuals and communities realistically can do to heal themselves.

If Christian belief and practice were to offer these services to contemporary individuals and communities, or even to whole societies, it is conceivable that the primitive could be allowed to return in medicinal rather than toxic doses. In a personal as well as a collective descent into hell, individuals and their societies could be expected to take responsibility for their ancient hatreds and longings. These emotions do indeed keep polluting the wells of public discourse and feeding hopes for collective triumph and vindication against a wide range of real and imaginary enemies. To expose them in a process of personal and collective self-examination might prevent irresponsible leadership from mobilizing them for political purposes. To fail in this endeavor is to hold the door open for a wide variety of racial, ethnic and religious mullahs of the sort periodically generated at least in American society.

Unless it is radically reformed, however, Christianity represents a very poor guide or antidote to the primitive. Here I will use Freud's own rather bleak assessment of Christianity as a guide to some of the primitive elements in Christianity itself: elements that make the Christian faith more like the disease than the cure. In doing so I will be arguing that the time has come for a psychoanalytic reassessment of the Christian faith: one that would enable Christianity to be a guide to the depths of the psyche rather than a repository of magical and grandiose thinking, old grievances and impossible hopes for restoration and victory. Let us begin with Freud's own assessment:

> In certain respects the new religion was a cultural regression as compared with the older Jewish religion; this happens regularly when a new mass of people of a lower cultural level effects an invasion or is admitted into an older culture. The Christian religion did not keep to the lofty heights of spirituality to which the Jewish religion had soared. The former was no longer strictly monotheistic; it took over from the surrounding peoples numerous symbolical rites, re-established the great mother goddess, and found room for many deities of polytheism in an easily recognizable disguise, though in subordinate positions. Above all it is not inaccessible, as the Aton religion and the subsequent Mosaic religion had been, to the penetration of superstitions, magical and mystical elements which proved a great hindrance to the spiritual development of the two following millennia.[1]

This is not the place to engage in religious apologetics of one sort or another, and certainly a comparative and historical study of Judaism and Christianity with regard to their polytheistic and magical tendencies would be well beyond anything that I might attempt here. However, it is worth taking the time in this chapter to explore some of the implications of Freud's argument for the question that I have raised, that is whether Christianity is a reliable guide to the primitive and allows it to return in ways that are relatively conducive to personal and collective maturity.

Freud's argument against the role of Christianity as a spiritual guide goes deeper than his recognition that the Christian religion has promoted a return to polytheism, the adoration of the mother, and magical thinking. He also notes that Christianity itself originates in a founding event in which an earthly son, claiming to represent the heavenly father, is murdered. It is a murder like that of Moses, which Freud believes to have occurred regardless of the ambiguity of the scriptural record on this point. That is, the Christian faith heralds a return of the primitive revolt of the brothers against patriarchal authority, disguised as a murder of the son. The son who is murdered, however, claims to represent the father or even to be at one with him. The crucifixion is patricide.

It is no secret that the Israel that gave birth to the Christian faith was deeply engaged in fratricidal and occasionally patricidal conflict. In the centuries immediately prior to the birth of Christ and during the first half of the first century CE, Israel had been divided by civil wars in which the country itself was polarized between brothers competing with each other for the highest office. Often these conflicts required one side or the other to petition for outside help; thus Rome had been brought into the civil war that ended as Pompey invaded Jerusalem in 53 BCE. Not merely a heroic little country on the outskirts of the Roman empire, embattled in its defense against imperial power, Israel was itself divided in ways that gave the Roman imperium an opportunity and at times an invitation to invade. Brother was aligned against brother, and fathers and sons against one another, at the highest levels of the Herodian monarchy. Not long after the death of Jesus, the nation died in a civil war that was fratricidal from the outset.

It would therefore have been surprising if the early Christian community, at least in the Palestinian context, had not picked up elements of revolt against patriarchal authority and against brothers who assumed the mantle of patriarchal leadership. For the half century prior to the civil war of 66–73 CE that destroyed Jerusalem, Israel had embodied strong anti-patriarchal elements. The sons of Herod were accused of patricidal plots; the youth outside the Herodian palace tore down the Roman eagle over the gate of the Temple; the populace of Jerusalem protested en masse against the placement of imperial emblems in the Temple: to mention only a few of the events that might have stimulated old impulses on the part of the younger generation to replace the rule of the patriarchs with that of a fraternal order. Other conditions were also conducive to the return of primitive, rebellious impulses, especially the prevalence of crowds in which the individual's own identity and sense of responsibility were merged with that of a larger and more volatile collective. These are conditions very much like those that Freud considers to be conducive to the return of repressed elements from the unconscious: a relaxation of controls on primitive impulses that are being strengthened.[2] It would therefore be surprising if early Christianity had not embodied some of these earlier, revolutionary and patricidal impulses.

Certainly the sense of possibility was therefore reaching new heights as these primitive rivalries were remembered and re-enacted in Palestinian streets and in the countryside during the first seven decades of the first century CE. Dreams of a messianic kingdom returned in force, as did the memory of ancient grievances against alien rule. All the dangers of a return to the primitive that I mentioned at the beginning of this chapter were evident in the first-century civil conflicts of Israel. No wonder, then, that the Christian faith embodies the seditious and rebellious impulses of the brothers united against patriarchal rule, just as it embraces a hope of an impossible but imminent future and rekindles the memory of old battles against ancient enemies. The most ancient of these enemies, of course, was Satan, the bestial image of the father endowed with magical properties and the ability to possess or even destroy the soul.

The memory of these early revolts and primitive murders lives on, Freud would argue, not only in the cultural memories constantly revived and re-enacted through Christian rites, but in the individual's unconscious. There, if we are to follow Freud, lie traces of the primitive murders, as surely as there can be found in the psyches of animals real but unconscious traces of the primitive past. The dog never forgets the wolf, any more than the Christian fully forgets the patricide.

If it were not for these traces of collective memory in the individual unconscious, Freud goes on to suggest, there would be no need for the people to resurrect a figure who fills in all the qualities of the ancient but murdered father: resoluteness of will, kindness, a preference for his own dear children, a willingness to defend his convictions to the end, along with a certain fear-invoking tendency toward primitive rage.[3] There is something omniscient and omnipotent about such a Führer, but also something demonic. We can now better understand Freud's own fascination with Machiavelli's statue of Moses with the law tablets in his hands and traces of horns on his forehead: the father-figure revealed as satanic even in the act of laying down the law. He was a proto-Führer: powerful, insisting on the letter of the law, and yet full of destructive rage.

If Nazism was fundamentally anti-Christian as well as anti-Jewish, it was because the primitive aspects of Christianity had been finally replaced by Reformed Christianity and needed a new way to return. To be sure, Freud argued that Christianity originally had been a return to some of the more primitive aspects of faith that had been displaced by Jewish religion, for example, adoration of the mother, magic, polytheism and the revolt of the brothers against patriarchal authority. However, Christianity later became a major force for secularization in its prophetic attack on religious deviance and on indigenous communities of faith. Thus Freud argues that the Nazi movement itself was a return to primitive loyalties that had long been suppressed by imperial Christianity: 'The hatred for Judaism is at bottom hatred for Christianity, and it is not surprising that the German national socialist religion finds such clear expression in the hostile treatment of both.'[4]

It is important to understand why it is that Freud felt the Nazi movement to be hostile to the Church not simply as a rival source of authority but for deeply entrenched historical reasons. For Freud, current sufferings often represent a repetition of earlier injuries, and the primitive therefore returns with a vengeance for long-remembered injustices and ills. However, when the primitive returns, it may find a new target that resembles but also differs from the source of the original conflict. It is therefore not surprising that he argued a similar case with regard to German anti-Semitism:

> We must not forget that all the peoples who now excel in the practice of anti-Semitism became Christians only in relatively recent times, sometimes forced to it by bloody compulsion. One might say they are all 'badly christened'; under the thin veneer of Christianity that have remained what their ancestors were, barbarically polytheistic. They have not yet overcome their grudge against the new religion which was forced on them, and they have projected it on to the source from which Christianity came to them.[5]

Anyone who has read Richard Fletcher's superb new history of Western Christianity, *The Barbarian Conversion*, would know precisely what Freud had in mind.[6] Certainly the Anglo-Saxons were forced to accept 'peace and the sacraments' at the point of a Carolingian sword wielded by Christian missionaries. It was St. Boniface, among others, who pacified these barbarian peoples on what was then the fringe of the Carolingian empire. The Serbs and the Basques proved more resistant, as did the men from the north who finally slew Boniface. These early European *conquistadores* may well have been responsible for the long-standing German paranoia about invasion and domination by alien peoples. It is a memory that may have taken a number of forms, for example, in hope for an apocalyptic redeemer who would teach Rome a lesson and restore to Germany her ancient purity and territorial boundaries.[7] No doubt much of this suspicion of alien influences found its target in the Jewish population. Freud's point goes deeper, however, in that it calls to mind what may well have been this historical memory of being conquered and converted by force: 'poorly christened,' to use Freud's euphemism.

If Christianity now faces a rebellion from elements of a culture that have long been suppressed and that now seek to turn the historical tables, such a punishment is quite fitting, given what Freud saw as the early Christians' re-enactment of the original crime of the brothers against patriarchal authority. Indeed, the early Christian movement may have been part of a similar revolt by peoples who had been forced to convert to the Jewish religion under the more aggressive Hasmoneans. Galileans themselves had probably been forced to convert; at least they harbored their own form of nationalist or populist yearnings and were in revolt during the civil war that finally destroyed Jerusalem.

The point is simply that the return of suppressed possibilities, for example, ethnic nationalism and anti-patriarchal, fraternal revolts, would be a fitting problem for the Christian Church to have, given its origins in such rebellion and its later adaptation for use as a colonizing force. During the time of the Jesus movement and in the decades leading up to the civil war, there were recurrent outbreaks of Jewish nationalism, messianic expectation and apocalyptic hope for an historical triumph over ancient enemies. In these aspirations it was the past that was coming back in the form of the future: a new messiah like a son of David; a new prophet like the prophets of old; a son of the patriarchs who could institute a new brotherhood of universal scope and significance. Old grievances, a sense of historical injustice and aspirations long delayed required a new Abel who could judge Israel herself along with the nations of the world. These were the forms of the primitive that returned, sometimes with a vengeance, during the first century and again early in the second. No wonder that the primitive, as it returned, brought with it a sense of heightened possibility for a universal community as well as grandiose dreams of national glory. After two thousand years, it is not surprising to find the churches beleaguered by the very primitive forces that their faith once embodied but finally – under the influence of reform and their own secular tendencies – excluded.

Our task here is to remember the form that the primitive once took in Christian literature and in the Christian imagination. To recover these elements of our heritage, to make them as much a matter of common language as the proverbial 'Freudian slip,' would be an important step to taking the mystery and some of the destructive potency away from the primitive and often unconscious depths of popular and personal imagination.

No less so than ancient Palestine, modern societies are affected by primitive and repressed elements of the personal and collective psyche. Imagine desire as a river that continually flows out from the pool of the unconscious and streams over land while mixing with water from other sources. Sometimes the river stagnates and becomes polluted; at other times it is a torrent that overflows the boundaries set for it and destroys habitations along its course. Now imagine a people seeking to establish a city on an island in the middle of that same river. They must keep the unconscious stream at bay while still incorporating its vitality. They must embody, so to speak, the excluded possibilities of primitive desire in a way that establishes rather than destroys the city. They therefore name the city for a savage virgin, whose relics are buried in the city's own foundations.

The story comes from Dante's 'Inferno,' and I will return to it later in this chapter. For the moment it stands as an analogy for the psychoanalytic understanding of social life as being built on very primitive foundations: unfulfilled, destructive and erotic desire. While they remain savage, these foundations are purified by memory and made safe by tradition. In this disguised and sanctified form, these primitive sources of social vitality may occasionally overflow their banks and disrupt the life of the larger society;

they may also become mixed with other sources of inspiration and authority, and they may even stagnate and become polluted.

The city's foundations, since they contain relics of primitive emotions that are warlike and erotic, are therefore not only a source of great energy and vitality but of great potential self-destruction. The psyche, Freud once argued, seeks at some level to dissolve the distinctions that separate it from the rest of the world; the animate seeks to resolve itself back into the inanimate from which it came.[8] The river of the unconscious, as it were, seeks to overflow its banks and become merged with other streams and with the land itself.

For Freud, then, there is more than a mere analogy between individual and mass psychology; there is a certain correspondence between the two. The 'earliest impressions ... manifest themselves later in an obsessive fashion ... We feel that the same must hold good for the earliest experiences of mankind.'[9] Even allowing for the wide range of differences among societies and for the effects of various kinds of social organization, Freud finds a fundamental tendency to self-destruction in societies as different from one another as Nazi Germany and ancient Egypt. Indeed, his *Moses and Monotheism*, on which I am once again drawing in this discussion, was written as he witnessed the explosion of internal hatred in Nazi Germany, the destruction of the Jews, and the beginning of the inevitable destruction of the nation itself. Freud found in ancient Israel as well as in modern Germany a sometimes extreme ambivalence to higher authority. It is an ambivalence, he argued, that shows itself in a sometimes slavish dependence on – as well as in a sometimes murderous hatred for – patriarchal authority.

The pretensions of a people or of a nation to superiority, to exclusive and superior revelation, and to a right to rule over all other nations, if only at the end of history, will need to be demystified and discarded. If there is to be a way to prevent future holocausts, then, it will have to follow the same difficult path into the unconscious as psychoanalysis itself. How else can one explain or hope to transcend the strange mixture of grandiosity and submissiveness that characterized not only Germans, both Nazi and Jewish, but also every other society based on reverence for and hatred of patriarchal authority? The primitive will always return; the only question is whether it will be an uninvited and intrusive guest or one whose place has already been prepared with the same thoroughness and care that the analyst uses in working with a patient. Speaking of the identity between the delusions of childhood and the perennial return of primitive experience, Freud went on to say:

> One result of this is the emergence of the conception of one great God. It must be recognized as a memory – a distorted one, it is true, but nevertheless a memory. It has an obsessive quality; it simply must be believed. As far as its distortion goes, it may be called a delusion; in so far as it brings to light something from the past, it must be called the truth.[10]

What is being brought back from the past is quite simply the primitive. At first it takes the form of a deadly combination. Freud finds in the Mosaic tradition 'the longing for the father that lives in each of us from his childhood days, for the same father whom the hero of legend boasts of having overcome.'[11] On the one hand is the longing for the omnipotent and omniscient, the caring and protective father; on the other hand is the perennial desire to take his place and to enjoy his prerogatives, which included a monopoly on women and the right to castrate, banish or kill his sons. If it were not for the rivalry of the sons with the father, they would not have to eliminate him, and if it were not for their longing for his return, they would not have to suffer guilt or to re-institute the father in the form of a brother who enjoys patriarchal authority over the brethren. Indeed, Freud argues that the beginnings of a moral order, of incest taboos, and of the sacred itself can be found in the need of the brothers to re-institute a form of patriarchal authority after they had successfully eliminated the father himself.[12]

The primitive, for Freud, thus comprises a wide range of instinctual desires, many of them incestuous or aggressive. He argues that primitive human beings failed to distinguish clearly between what was human and what belongs to the animal kingdom.[13] Indeed we still refer to 'animal spirits' as a source of primitive vitality that may energize or disrupt the larger society. Thus it is not surprising that he finds the return of the primitive father necessary if the brothers are not to fight with one another over these prerogatives and satisfactions. One form of the primitive, the powerful father, is required to protect the psyche and the community against another form of the primitive, which is powerful and even overwhelming desire.[14]

There is more, however, to the primitive than the longing for the father or hatred for him; more to it than the return of primitive desire. For Freud the primitive also consists of the earliest experiences of the child, at a time when sexual desire and aggressiveness are poorly separated, and when early impressions often wound the child's own sense of being lovable and important.[15] Because societies require these early sexual and aggressive impulses to be repressed even while they are maturing, children undergo a latency period that is the breeding ground for neurosis. It is a time when the child feels what he or she is not yet entitled to acknowledge or express, let alone to satisfy. Thus neurosis develops, and it is part of the most primitive human condition. It is not surprising, then, for the primitive to return in the form of a grandiose sense of entitlement to satisfactions that the individual is as yet ill-prepared to command or enjoy. To return for a moment to Dante's imagery, there is a 'savage virgin' embodied in the foundations of every human community.

For Freud the secrets of the formation of neuroses also reveal the ways in which social character itself forms and develops.[16] However, the links between personal and social delusions are not always clear. Indeed, Freud seems to grasp a bit wildly for explanations for the admittedly uncanny resemblance between mass and individual psychology. At times he seems to think it sufficient simply to argue that these ambivalent tendencies have their origin in childhood; it is no wonder that they therefore reappear in every generation or take form in a wide range of social institutions. Because they are perennial, these grandiose and destructive fantasies will be variously translated from childhood into the life of institutions, communities, societies and nations. If, however, there is a universal tendency toward certain kinds of neurotic dependence on authority, how are we to explain the differences between communities and nations in this regard?

When it comes to explaining differences among various societies, as we have seen, Freud bases his argument on the specific tradition that he finds at the heart of Israelite religion: the Mosaic tradition that he considered to be a return to the original, Egyptian religious culture under Ikhnaton.[17] It was from that source, he argued, that Israel derived its ancient monotheism and from which it learned to consider itself to be a nation superior to all others with whom it was competing for physical and symbolic space in the Middle East. The exclusive monotheism of Ikhnaton ultimately was the foundation for the Israelite belief in a God who was not only superior to all other gods but who alone could be considered divine. Such a God required exclusive and absolute allegiance and obedience from his people, in return for which he gave them a sense of exclusive and absolute uniqueness and superiority over all other peoples of the world. Thus Freud finds that there is an important cultural difference between Israel and other nations, whereas his theory would have him look for uniformities among cultures in their ambivalent regard for authority and in their latent demands for impossible satisfactions.

There is more to Freud's historical argument than a mere narrative of how Israel's origins in Egypt predisposed it to a particular set of national illusions. Embedded in this historical account of national differences is an evolutionary rather than psychoanalytic perspective: a Darwinian notion of the survival of the fittest. He speaks of 'a special psychical fitness in the mass which had become the Jewish people that it could bring forth so many persons who were ready to take upon themselves the burden of the Mosaic religion for the reward of believing that their people was a chosen one and perhaps for other benefits of a similar order.'[18] The notions of a 'special psychical fitness' have an uncomfortable resemblance to racial theories of superiority, of course, and it is perhaps fortunate that Freud does not develop the point much further.

Faced with a tension, then, between his general theory of the primitive origins of all social systems and the rather specific manifestations of his theory in the particular history of Israel, Freud falls back on anthropological sources that he knows to have been criticized or even discredited. These sources argued for a widespread institution of kingship that was based on the sacrifice of the king himself. It did not matter to him, he said later in the discussion, that anthropologists no longer believed that such an institution existed. It was his 'right' to select from sources whatever suited the theory that he was propounding on clinical grounds.

If there is a scandal, so to speak, in Freud's thinking, it is that the collective unconscious of a particular people endows it with its own peculiar version of general tendencies, found in all cultures, to transmit a primitive past. Certainly his logic required him also to believe in the inheritance of social characteristics. That there was a collective unconscious that harbored particularly primitive passions and delusions Freud had no doubt:

> Our supposition was that the religion of Moses was discarded and partly forgotten and that, later on, it forced itself on the notice of people as a tradition. I make this assumption that this process was the repetition of an earlier one. When Moses gave to his people the conception of an Only God it was not an altogether new idea, for it meant the reanimation of primeval experience in the human family that had long ago faded from the conscious memory of mankind. The experience was such an important one, however, and had produced, or at least prepared, such far-reaching changes in the life of man that, I cannot help thinking, it must have left some permanent trace in the human soul – something comparable to a tradition.[19]

Ultimately, I would argue, it was Freud's own self-knowledge that convinced him that humans were at heart regicides and patricides as well as all too willing servants of higher authority. He had found this fatal ambivalence in his own psyche through the analysis of his dreams.[20]

What is needed, clearly, is the sort of social theory that I was beginning to sketch in the second chapter. It is a theory that accounts for the construction and the return of the primitive according to the ways in which particular societies include and exclude certain possibilities. For instance, societies that wish to prevent their sons and brothers from satisfying their erotic desires with women belonging to the same family, community or society must direct those desires outward; that was Freud's point about patriarchal societies requiring exogamy. Thus certain possibilities are excluded and defined as 'primitive.' Women from the outside thus come to represent alien sources of interest, inspiration and authority, and they can introduce unwanted genes into the patrilineal pool: necessary and yet suspect, desirable but threatening.

Similarly, societies need to create a spirit of unselfish and warlike enthusiasm for killing enemies while making sure that those aggressions do not find targets within the system. To create and externalize violence is a major and continuing project for many societies, but it is a dangerous project if only because it is not always possible to inculcate unquestioning obedience to the father or to higher authority along with a warlike disposition. If too much submissiveness is developed, violence may well be directed internally toward the obedient and helpless. However, if warlike dispositions prevail, a society may self-destruct from patricidal or fratricidal conflict. Israel at various points of its history could illustrate either set of outcomes.

Societies will inevitably construe certain possibilities as beyond the pale, where they seem neither feasible nor morally acceptable. Attributed therefore to the environment, they may remain embodied in religious language, whether in the form of prophecy and apocalyptic language, or in the form of liturgical enactment under carefully controlled conditions. These forbidden possibilities were the staple of what Martha Himmelfarb has called 'tours of hell': a literary form prevalent throughout ancient Greece and Israel, with precedents in ancient Egypt and Mesopotamia.[21] These excluded possibilities constitute a potential that the society can understand, rehearse, and on occasion, if necessary, include in its own repertoire of sexuality and violence. There may come a time when millennial beliefs justify the acting-out of violence and of sexual desire in ways that in ordinary times would have been prohibited. Holy wars are fought; orgies carried out. The time for Rapture finally comes. What had been relegated to an unthinkable or rejected past returns in the form of a future that in the meantime could only have been anticipated with the greatest desire and apprehension. It is a future that sometimes appears in apocalyptic form rather than as a 'tour of hell.'

What seems like a term referring to space, the 'environment,' really therefore refers to the passage of time. What is excluded as a possibility as one gets older and grows up is relegated to a past that is regarded as infantile and even primitive, children being sometimes regarded as little savages as well as proto-adults. Conversely, from the child's point of view, early dreams of rivaling the father and triumphing over him for the mother's affections are relegated to an environment of impossible but not unimaginable outcomes. They represent a future that, because its initial content is repressed, returns disguised in whatever form the sacred may give it: visions of ecstatic reunion, of victory over enemies, of hunting conquests – the animal being a substitute for the father, or other dreams of comparable glory.

The excluded possibility that has been relegated to the past may return slowly over the course of the individual's development or as the society in question adapts to new opportunities and threats from its environment. However, the past, formerly excluded, possibility may return abruptly should individuals take their character, so to speak, in their own hands, whether by following alien authorities, subscribing to dissident leadership, or rejecting prescribed models for adulthood. Magical thinking, a refusal to accept limitations, homosexual libido, a penchant for enchantment and arrested development: these are only some of the elements of the unconscious that come to light in a search for the primitive aspects of the personal and collective psyche. Under these conditions the past may return in the form of a future that has been envisioned as a day of judgement for the settling of old scores or for liberating the society from various forms of what Freud called instinctual renunciation: an apocalyptic version of hell.

We must not overlook the possibility, furthermore, that behind such perennial striving is the attempt to recover a self that was lost in moments of trauma. The memory of sexual abuse, as I will later argue, is often buried too deeply in the psyche to be recovered, and with it is lost the part of the self that was immobilized and numbed as an emotional defense against that abuse. Indeed, one may simply have to accept that a part of the self is entombed in such memories and can never be recovered.[22] Such moments may also be traumatic and toxic to the self, not only because of the abuse, but because of the individual's own rage that, deprived of an outlet, visits on the self some of the destruction intended for another.

That is, societies may be able to enter into the realm of excluded possibility in the same way that individuals can return to the areas of their psyches that they have repressed. In making such a return to excluded possibility, societies will no doubt uncover earlier, perhaps grandiose and vindictive imaginings, dreams of national glory, beliefs in racial entitlements, memories of ancient suffering and loss, and vital energies long since suppressed in the service of more pragmatic or rational pursuits. This is what has long been understood as a descent into hell. As a national pursuit it is better undertaken with care under trained leadership. Otherwise, as in fascist Germany, it may become a national pursuit undertaken by another sort of leadership altogether.

## Notes

1 Sigmund Freud, *Moses and Monotheism*, translated by Katherine Jones (1939), New York: Vintage Books, p. 122.
2 Ibid., p. 121.
3 Ibid., pp. 140–41.
4 Ibid., p. 117.
5 Ibid., 1939, pp. 116–17.
6 Richard Fletcher (1997), *The Barbarian Conversion. From Paganism to Christianity*, New York: Henry Holt and Co. I am relying on Fletcher throughout this paragraph.
7 See, for example, Norman Cohn's discussion of the *Syballine Oracles* in *The Pursuit of the Millennium*, revised and expanded edition (1970), New York: Oxford University Press, pp. 71 ff.
8 I have discussed this aspect of Freud's thought at some length in *Time Exposure*, Oxford and New York: Oxford University Press, 2001.
9 Freud, op. cit., p. 167.
10 Ibid.
11 Ibid., p. 140.
12 Ibid., p. 104.
13 Ibid.

14 Ibid., p. 152.
15 Ibid., p. 93.
16 Ibid., p. 95.
17 Ibid., p. 141.
18 Ibid., p. 142.
19 Ibid., pp. 166–7.
20 See Note 2, Chapter 4.
21 Martha Himmelfarb (1983), *Tours of Hell. An Apocalyptic Form in Jewish and Christian Literature*, Philadelphia: The University of Pennsylvania Press.
22 See, for instance, the discussion in Shengold, *Soul Murder, Ch 10*.

# Chapter 4

# Recovering the Primitive: Dante's Descent into Hell

The capacity of Christianity to speak of excluded possibilities in ways that make the unfamiliar and threatening seem relatively imaginable, and the enticing but prohibited seem understandable if illegitimate, has long depended, as I have suggested, on its capacity to talk about hell. If hell is the land of excluded possibilities, much has depended on whether the vision of hell was informed by popular imagination or by official concerns with maintaining control over local devotions and behavior. For instance, one document that we will consider, *The Vision of Wetti*, like *Piers Plowman*, has a populist flair to it, with much attention being paid to official misdemeanors, but it also showed signs of official editing that reminded the hearer of his or her penitential obligations. As Martha Himmelfarb has pointed out in her study of 'tours of hell' in the ancient Near East, the satisfaction of watching sinners hanging by their offending body parts was a staple of authorized versions of the netherworld. Even the pleasure of imagining certain possibilities requires that the devil of higher authority, so to speak, be paid its due.

As the Church's interest in hell became increasingly disciplinary, intrusive and inquisitorial, the literary form of religious imagination remained open to the primitive. In Dante's 'Inferno' we can find a cast of the characters that in his time had been placed beyond the pale of civilization. Indeed we shall find there suicides and sodomists, along with a reassertion that it is a divine, as it were imperial, decree rather than any more natural or negotiable fate that lands one in hell. However, these attempts to recover possibilities excluded by the civilization do not begin to touch what Freud had in mind when he referred to a tradition: a repressed memory that nonetheless lived on in the soul and, to some degree, in the collective psychology of the people themselves. This repressed element is something more than the animal or sub-human rather than civilized and humane. It is what to an historical observer would seem primitive in the sense of primal: a memory of earlier experience that had been too powerful and intense either to bear or wholly to forget.

In the 'Inferno' we find precisely such references to the primitive as an antique past that is a source both of perennial vitality and of abhorrence at perennially destructive passions. This is the primitive in Freud's sense: a living but partially repressed memory of pagan origins that still upset the civility of the city even while these origins are its foundation. That is, in Dante's return to the primitive in hell we find the same mixture of longing and denial, of ancient desire and primal hatred, that Freud found in the longing for the primitive father who had been at once an object of adoration and of murderous passions in the primitive clan. There we find Dante longingly viewing the possibilities and pitying the people, the passions and the loves that have been excluded. Indeed, he chafes at the bit of the reality-principle exemplified in Virgil. In hell the old passions remain turbulent, even when they are forced to remain hopeless and are placed in the world of repressed collective memory.

In Freud's theory, as we have noted, what is repressed in collective memory is the experience of being under the power of an all-knowing, all-providing father or king who was the object of both adoration and hatred. To provide for oneself, to claim foreknowledge and to act as one's own provider would therefore be an act of lese-majesté. It is the father, and the father alone, who has the ability to foretell the future and the authority to provide for his people. That is the source of his appeal, of course, but it is also the reason for the profound ambivalence of popular feeling toward a patriarchal authority.

To know and provide for the future is the power of a deity and of kings who seemed to their people to be divine. Among the damned, therefore, Dante describes the fate of those who took up divination and thus sought to know and perhaps even alter the future. These unhappy creatures are fated to look backwards; Dante pictures them as having their heads turned around 180 degrees, so that they continually see only where they have been and can thus only remember and regret their desires and presumptions. These creatures are epiphanies of hell itself as a place where one continues to long for and regret a past even though one knows that it is too late for those longings to be fulfilled or for the past to be undone. Their future is their past.

It is not too late, of course, for Dante's hearers to recover the memory of their own imagined presumptions, their ancient hatreds and their longing for a supreme, fatherly authority. As we shall see, Dante reminds the people of Florence that their own city is filled with primitive and warlike passions that remain unsatisfied until they are quenched in the river of hell, where it is too late fully to satisfy them, even though in hell they can never be forgotten. That hell is precisely where Freud places the living memories of half-forgotten events and figures that, like the king, are larger than life and, precisely because their memory is repressed, remain a stimulus to the grandiose imagination.

Thus in Dante, as in Freud, we have these surprising references to memories that are collective and at least half-forgotten if not wholly repressed. They survive in myths that are popular but whose meaning has largely been forgotten. They survive in statues of warlike figures: mementoes of a history that lives in the present in the form of warlike passions that are barely covered by a veneer of civility. In calling this a collective unconscious I do not mean to invoke the mysteries of Jungian psychology but only to point to a fact of social life that is relatively widespread. Wherever a cross is burned, for instance, some people remember a recent and painful chapter in American society, but few remember the lighted crosses on the hills of Scotland that announced earlier wars for blood, race and soil. Few who celebrate the possibility of a once and future king will remember Arthur, but the legend lives on in games and entertainment whose origin in battles for a people and a place in the West of England have long been forgotten.

Thus a king who is imagined to be more than a match for death is not unusual or the invention of a medieval poet's imagination. He alone, because he is all knowing, can foresee the moment of his death and, because he is larger than life in the collective imagination, this is a king who will eventually triumph over death. His memory, long repressed, is itself bound to return because it is exempt from the penalties of death and lives on in a cultural imagination that feeds on images of immortality. However, in Dante's 'Inferno,' there are always rivals and imposters: lesser kings and chiefs, and other ordinary mortals, who presume to foresee the day of their death and seek to avoid it. They are a travesty of the earthly king-made-divine, and they must suffer punishment at the hands of the king who is imagined truly to be all-knowing, all-providing and immortal. Impostors to kingship inevitably suffer punishment from the repressed memory of a king who is death on pretenders to his throne. That is precisely why, as Freud put it, the memory of the slain father and king returns to wreak vengeance on the brothers who have usurped his authority.

Such a king who brooks no final opposition was Aton, Freud noted, but Freud also, as we have seen, argued that in Greek cultural history the divine king whose memory was repressed and who yet lived on in the collective imagination was Minos. This ancient king presided over a civilization whose glory had not yet been equaled and over an empire that for centuries after its fall fed the popular imagination of a reign that could triumph over all opposition and death. It is not surprising, then, to find in Dante's 'Inferno' a mention of this ancient, mythic ruler, Minos, who seizes all those who seek to usurp his power and to foresee the day of their own deaths. For example, in the twentieth canto Dante refers to one Amphiarus, a king who had joined the battle against the city of Thebes only to flee the scene when he foresaw his own death:

> 'Why are you leaving the war, //
> Amphiarus,' the others shouted, 'what place /

Are you rushing to?' as he plunged down the crevice /
to Minos, who seizes all. See Amphiaurus //
Making his shoulders his breast; because his purpose /
Was seeing too far ahead, he looks behind /
And stumbles backwards,

Canto XX.33–39[1]

Since the crime is to try to foresee and forestall the moment of one's death, the punishment is that one must forever see that one is too late. The preoccupation with death is thus 'displaced' from the future to the past. Anxiety at the prospect of being late (both tardy and dead) becomes chronic remorse over the fact that one is already too late to change the past. It is a fitting punishment for those who have presumed on the prerogatives of the king made divine, who alone has foreknowledge and can transcend the passage of time. He is, as Freud has reminded us, Father Time, and the rebellious sons are doomed to be punished by the one whose place they have sought to take.

In this split-off fashion, the memory of ancient patricidal passion operates as a collective symptom of a deeply held and widespread cultural memory that has long been suppressed in its original form and can surface only in one or another cultural disguise.[2]

It would be a mistake to underestimate the importance of this passage on Amphiarus and Minos. In the portion we have just quoted from Canto XX about the fate of Amphiarus, the voice is that of Virgil in 'his longest speech in the "Inferno," ' (The Notes by Nicole Pinsky to Canto XX.83–84).[3] His tones are clearly those of a paternal authority opposed to Dante's sentimental and unrealistic compassion for one who, like Amphiaraus, sought to see 'too far ahead' and now 'looks behind/And stumbles backwards.' In fact, Virgil scolds Dante for weeping at the sight of those with their heads twisted backwards and asks him:

'Do you suppose/You are above with the other fools even yet?
Here, pity lives when it is dead to these.
Who could be more impious than one who'd dare
To sorrow at the judgment God decrees?'

Canto XX.26–30[4]

One has to descend into hell to understand the real situation of humans *vis-à-vis* ultimate reality. There, pity can only survive when it is 'dead' to feelings of compassion for sinners such as these, whose offense is that they have rebelled against the authority that limits human life to an uncertain and unknowable span of time. It is an offense against the authority of the primal father to be one's own source of providence. Thus, in Virgil's reprimand, we have a vestige not only of the patriarchal but of the bureaucratic, even the imperial, understanding of the underworld as a place to which one is summoned or banished by heavenly authority. The sight of one who sought to usurp the prerogatives of Father Time can only be contemplated with judgement, not pity.

Remember that Freud emphasized the ambivalence of the sons' attitudes toward the father. The sons are both devout and rebellious, adoring and seditious toward the patriarch. Their primitive hatred is thus matched by a primal, filial love. Much of the spiritual tension in the 'Inferno' therefore lies in the conflict between Dante's tendencies toward rebellion and obedience. On the one hand we sense Dante's compassion for unfortunate rebels; on the other we find Dante submitting dutifully to Virgil's reminders of the limits set by nature and God, that is, by reality itself. Translated into the imaginary setting of a descent into hell, Dante's conflict becomes a contest between the longing to fulfill ancient desire and thus to recover lost parts of the self, and the knowledge that it is too late to do so. Thus, when Virgil criticizes Dante for being confused in his pity, Virgil is trying to remind him of more than one barrier. The first separates the living from the dead. Thus Dante's pity for the dead can only live 'when it is dead to these' souls with their heads turned backwards. The second boundary that Virgil is asserting is the line separating father from son. Reality, as defined by patriarchal authority, and the longings of the son, however understandable they may be, do not fight in a divine scheme because patricidal fantasy has been excluded once and for all.

For a while Dante appears willing to confirm the importance of paternal authority as well as to respect the boundary between the living and the dead; here is his reply to Virgil's speech:

> 'Master, your speech inspires such certainty
> And confidence that any contradiction
> Of what you say would be dead coals to me,'

> Canto XX.85–86[5]

The words of Virgil have thus marked the difference between life and death. To oppose them would be to try to breathe fire into coals whose life had gone out of them. Dante thus signifies that he knows when it is too late for more passion to be spent on a hopeless quest: hopeless not only because the object of the quest is dead, but hopeless because of the authority of the father. Virgil marks out as fools those who waste their pity on the departed. Belatedly, Dante appears willing to exclude the possibility of a vital relation to the dead. These dead, at least, are to be forever beyond the pale of human compassion. They represent possibilities that are always and everywhere to be excluded: the primitive in all its hopelessness. One does not have to strain to detect here the vestiges of what Freud described as the reign of the primitive father, who enjoyed a monopoly on the objects of male affection and thus excluded a wide range of passions from possible satisfaction.

At the risk of too much repetition, let me say again that the excursion into a world of excluded possibility is a rebellion against the reality-principle in any society, whether or not that society is dominated by patriarchal authority. Granted that Dante's illustrations of chronic and perpetual rebellion focus on those who like the king stood up against the patriarch of all patriarchs and thus incurred the wrath of Zeus. Nonetheless, his more general point remains the same: to descend into hell is the ultimate act of sedition against the limits set by any social system. It is also the most pitiable, since the individual is engaging in a hopeless and self-defeating struggle not only against social authority but against ultimate reality. It is not only patriarchal authority that excludes such possibilities; it is life itself, in the form of death, that puts satisfaction forever out of the reach of some hatreds and loves.

There are at least two Dantean voices: one clearly articulating the conventional notions of what is possible and permitted; the other articulating reprehensible possibility. In an earlier canto, for instance, Dante had portrayed the problem of continuing to sustain moribund affections. Canto XV begins with a reference to strong barriers that separate the sea from the land. Thus we are prepared for a discussion of those who violate natural boundaries, fail to respect natural limits and limitations, and cause pollution by mixing what should be kept separate. Indeed this canto is about one who violated at least two natural limits, gender and time: one Brunetto who is a bit of a soothsayer as well as one who has had intercourse with men. Dante as poet casts himself in the role of one for whom the future remains relatively opaque and for whom natural limits are sacrosanct: sodomists and soothsayers are possibilities for human development that are morally, if not actually, excluded. However, Dante as wanderer embodies excluded possibility, as in this explanation to Brunetto of how he (Dante) came to be traveling through Hell while still quite alive:

> 'In the bright light above,' I answered him,
> 'I came into a valley and lost my way,
> Before my age had reached its ripening time –'

> Canto XV.43–45[6]

Thus Dante's affection for Brunetto afflicts him (Dante) with anguish over the fact that the flow of time cannot be reversed. Indeed, Dante's strong affection for the dead, and for Brunetto in particular, is the vehicle for a moribund desire for eternity:

> 'Could I have everything for which I long,
> You would not still endure this banishment

Away from human nature,' I replied.
'Your image – dear, fatherly, benevolent –
Being fixed inside my memory, has imbued
My heart: when in the fair world, hour by hour,
You taught me, patiently, it was you who showed
The way man makes himself eternal,'

Canto XV.75–82[7]

To be sure, Dante is not to be confused with those who take premature flight from the future only to be condemned to perennial retrospection. Nonetheless, his desire for fatherly love that would transcend the passage of time and death itself is evident in this passage; it is precisely the passion that Freud said humans never outgrow: the longing for a wise and protective father. It was Brunetto who had offered Dante the illusion that one could go on forever; Brunetto had 'showed/ The way man makes himself eternal.' Now it is too late for Dante to satisfy his affection for his deceased teacher. Indeed, it is possible that the loss of this 'father' (Brunetto) who had appeared to rise above time contributed to Dante's experience of entering a valley and losing his way before his own 'ripening time.'[8]

If Dante ever does experience the pangs of hell directly, rather than from the vantage-point of the poet or with the pilgrim's anticipation of later beatitude, it is in these verses. Here he is not viewing his relation to Brunetto under the aspect of eternity or looking forward to a holy reunion with him at the end of his journey. Instead, the hard fact of natural limits has placed an immovable, but to Dante an unacceptable, barrier between them: the gulf that separates the living from the dead. There are also other boundaries, allegedly natural ones, coded in natural law, that separate the human or natural from the sub-human and unnatural. These codes thus exclude certain forms of sexuality as being against the laws of nature.[9] Those boundaries are compromised, however, by the fact that Brunetto still lives in Dante's heart, even though he is dead and appears to have violated the laws of nature.[10] Thus it is too late for Dante either to satisfy his old affection for Brunetto or to rid himself of this moribund affection.

However, official guides to hell are often likely to view the damned with high or official disregard. Certainly from Dante's viewpoint, those who violate the boundaries of nature are a source of dangerous pollution. As if to underscore the importance of wasting no pity on those who would transcend the limits of time, Virgil recites a story about the foundation of his city, Mantua. (The story itself is another of Dante's inventions, since in the *Aeneid* Virgil himself comes up with a rather different account of Mantua's origin; see the note to Canto XX.83–84).[11] Dante has Virgil ascribe the founding of his birthplace to a people who sought a secure island in the midst of a marsh: 'with no lots or divination/They named it Mantua,' (Canto XX.80–81).[12] It is indeed an earthly city, but it is built on what Himmelfarb notes is an ancient metaphor for the netherworld itself, the swampy and low places into which one is most likely to sink: not a bad notion for the depths of the psyche as well as of despair.[13]

In the context of his speech about Mantua, Virgil describes a lake that manages to contain within its perimeter streams from 'a thousand sources,' and when these overflow a river is formed that, once it has joined the Po, 'Spreads to a marsh — in summer, sometimes fetid,' (Canto XX.57,70).[14] Once the river leaves the lake, its name changes, and when it mixes with the water of another river it becomes boundless and polluted. However, there is in this marsh the island to which I earlier referred, where a city was found that later became Virgil's birthplace. The speech of Virgil thus functions as an assertion of the rightness of natural boundaries; he has no sympathy, as we have seen, for those who, like soothsayers, transgress the confinements of time. Thus it is fitting that his speech includes a reminder of the natural boundaries of Italy to the north: '... Where a wall of mountains rises/To form fair Italy's border above Tirolo,' (Canto XX.55–56).[15]

There can be little doubt that Dante is here playing on the importance of social as well as natural boundaries in excluding dangerous, alien and polluting influences. However, the image of the city itself, built on the firm foundation of this island, is somewhat ambiguous, since it contains within itself a symbol of the primitive. Just as Florence contained the relics of a statue of Mars, so does Mantua contain the relics of a 'savage virgin' who lived there: Manto, after whom the city of Mantua itself was later named. That is, the city embodies the excluded possibility and thus enshrines the primitive. To be sure, the island in the marsh, on which the city was built, was 'A stretch of dry land, untilled, uninhabited:' clearly virgin territory, not only unspoiled but separate from the swampy surroundings where earth and water were unhappily mixed together. The purity of origin of that earthly city could hardly be more dramatic; indeed the city was built over the virgin's bones, themselves the emblem of ancestry and dryness, while the surrounding marsh is a sink-hole of unhappy mixtures. Even the virgin was, after all, a 'savage.' It is as if the city of Mantua stands as a classical model for social life in which the primitive is safely domesticated by being placed in the very foundation of the city, and all pollution, like the surrounding marsh, is wholly external. Thus Mantua could contain and purify the savage and in the process obtain from it not only a source of purity but of vital energy.

The collective unconscious, then, like the psyche of the individual, cannot always retain the past in the form of domesticated desire. Some passions are too powerful and destructive to be safely interred. For instance, like Mantua, Dante's own city, Florence, was founded on the primitive that had been partially but unsuccessfully excluded from its later, more civil institutions. Indeed, Dante's Florence stands as the social embodiment of the desire to continue to experience old passions even when it is too late to fulfill them. Speaking of a lost soul, a suicide in hell, Dante writes the first line of Canto XIV:

> *Compelled by the love I bear my native place,*
> I gathered the scattered sprays and gave them again
> To him who was already faint of voice,
>
> Canto XIV.1–2; emphasis added[16]

The 'scattered sprays' come from a bush described in the previous canto: the embodiment of a soul who had killed himself and is now ravaged by animals; he had been, like Dante, a citizen of Florence, and had described that ancient city as continuing to be ravaged by a civil war. The war had ancient and very primitive roots, stemming at least from the time in which Florence had left the worship of Mars for that of Christianity. In its depths, however, the city had retained a piece of an old statue of Mars, which was part of its continuing vitality as well as the core of the city's perennial martial passions (note to Canto XIII.134–142).[17] That relic was a sign of the continuing presence of the past and of the primitive in the life of the civilized and Christian city. Like so many of those whom Freud described, the Florentians were doomed to repeat the most unpleasant of past experiences.

The relic of the statue of Mars 'is what permits it to be rebuilt each time it is laid waste,' but it is also Mars that 'punishes Florence with constant war and fighting,' (note to Canto XIII.134–142).[18] That is indeed the primitive: a source of vital energies, and yet also a source of destructive passions. Indeed, Dante goes on to describe a scene of perpetual warfare and suffering, as flame falls continuously from the sky, mingling first with the air, the earth and sand, only to be quenched in the waters of a bloody creek. The appearance of the creek itself is heralded by Dante:

> 'In all that I have shown you,' my master said,
> 'Since first we entered through that open gate
> Whose threshold no one ever is denied,
> Nothing your eyes have seen is so worth note
> As this present stream which quenches in its flood
> All of the flames above it,'
>
> Canto XIV.69–74[19]

It is a river, Virgil later tells us, that flows from the Acheron, Styx and Phlegethon: a stream turned red and boiling by the passions that it 'quenches in its flood.' It is the river of time flowing through the 'realm of grief,' and it shows up not only in ancient Greek but also Jewish sources.[20] Like the city of Florence, that turned from Mars to John the Baptist, it contains old and destructive passions that keep it in turmoil because they are preserved rather than forgotten, even while it cools them slowly over time. It is only in purgatory, when at last the river finally flows into Lethe and offers forgetfulness, that 'repented guilt removed, souls gather//To cleanse themselves,' (Canto XIV.117–118).[21] Until then no old passion is forgotten, even though it is far too late for satisfaction.

## Notes

1 *The Inferno of Dante*, a new verse translation by Robert Pinsky with Notes by Nicole Pinsky, Foreword by John Freccero (1994), New York: The Noonday Press, Farrar, Straus and Giroux, p. 161.
2 In hell, the sympathies and passions of humans who defy the limits of time are the source of a number of perversions, none of them to Virgil's liking, although, as we have seen, Dante himself, as pilgrim, had some sympathy for the plight of the soothsayers who were compelled to look backwards as they walked awkwardly forward.
3 Ibid., p. 334.
4 Ibid., p. 159.
5 Ibid., p. 163.
6 Ibid., p. 121.
7 Ibid., p. 123.
8 Brunetto's banishment is not only from life but from 'human nature:' a clear reference, I would suggest, to Brunetto's sodomy as an unnatural breaking down of natural limits and barriers between men.
9 Freccero, John, *Notes*, pp. 327–328.
10 I say 'appears' to have violated the laws, since the offense is Dante's own invention; at least there is no other evidence for the attribution of sodomy to Brunetto (Note, Canto XV; Pinsky Ibid., p. 328).
11 *The Inferno of Dante*, op. cit., pp. 334–335.
12 Ibid., p. 163.
13 Martha Himmelfarb (1983), *Tours of Hell. An Apocalyptic Form in Jewish and Christian Literature*, Philadelphia: The University of Pennsylvania Press, pp. 107–8.
14 *The Inferno of Dante*, op. cit., pp. 161, 163.
15 Ibid., p. 161.
16 *The Inferno of Dante*, op. cit., p. 111; emphasis added.
17 Ibid., p. 326.
18 Ibid., p. 326.
19 Ibid., p. 115.
20 Himmelfarb, op. cit., p. 112.
21 *The Inferno of Dante*, op. cit., p. 117.

# Chapter 5

# Experiencing the Primitive

To experience the primitive is to find oneself in the grip of a passion or presence that seems to come from beyond oneself. Such an experience may come in events that seem, like lightning or falling in love, to be fortuitous, strange, unearthly, potent, momentous, revelatory, and thus from above. On the other hand, as in the case of witchcraft, the experience of the primitive may arise in relationships that are familiar, enduring, formative, and yet outside one's immediate influence. For the aboriginal, for instance, the ancestors have left their impression on the landscape, and their presence is felt as a sort of absence. To experience the primitive is to be haunted, as Linda Woodhead has put it, 'haunted by possibility.'

The same sense of being haunted by hitherto illegitimate or merely unprecedented or unimaginable possibility is likely to arise in any society in which those who are absent profoundly affect people. Even, or especially, in complex societies, cameras monitor the movements of the ordinary citizen, one becomes aware of unseen presences and of indirect surveillance. The lives of the rich and famous are exposed and explored in more interactive modes, for example, in on-line chat rooms and radio or television talk shows. The marketplace creates thousands who become addicted to the possibilities of on-line, independent investing, just as the internet creates the possibility of keeping intimate relationships alive by e-mail. Under these conditions the village church, the local sanctuary, is no longer able to monopolize the intimacies and attractions – or to forestall the dangers – offered in a social system whose physical and moral boundaries have become permeable to influences that no longer seem to be merely from the outside. The sense of presences that are simultaneously alien and distant but also familiar and intimate may make mundane events often seem to be as bewitched as they sometimes are in any so-called 'primitive' community. The immediacy of what hitherto has been thought to be beyond, and the opening-up of possibilities that hitherto had been considered impossible, constitute the experience of the primitive.

The primitive-modern thus lives in a world enchanted by presences that are more felt than visible, but that are nonetheless occasionally even seen and touched. Regardless of their occasional apparition, however, these presences are deeply internal to the individual psyche. They are an intimate part of the self, and, like the superego or like infantile desire, they thrive in the unconscious itself as well as in the more conscious levels of the psyche. That in itself is neither new or surprising. For instance, it has not been very long since people knew what it meant to be possessed by the alter egos, the doubles, or the familiars of witches or demons. Europeans in particular knew what it was like to have an incubus in bed: someone in the community who, by virtue of time and space, should have been elsewhere, but who instead seemed to be intimately with or within them. They knew what it was like to be possessed by those who, by reasons of their gender or social standing, should have been at a safe emotional remove, and they found themselves internally alive to the intentions or passions of those who were physically distant.

To experience the primitive, then, is to live in a social universe in which spiritual influences can travel freely and not only influence one's fortunes but inhabit one's inner self. Such experiences of the primitive then, as now, could be profoundly disturbing. No wonder people associated these familiars and alter egos with the power to communicate with the dead.[1] To be primitive, then, is like living in a virtual world controlled by cybernetic hackers intent on transmitting a virus to one's own memory.

To experience the primitive is thus to be in the presence and under the influence of another person regardless of the circumstances of time and space. It is the experience of the ecstatic, of being beside oneself, or of being captivated by the presence of another soul who seems to take precedence over one's own.[2] Thus shamans are thought to be able to be in two places at the same time; their souls, too, can travel. Like birds, they inhabit two dimensions and can be present even though they are absent in the flesh. That may be because they are the bearers of a spirit from the past or because they have incorporated the lasting presence of a temporary phenomenon, like a comet, whose uncanny and momentous influence endures long after its passing.

To experience the primitive one may feel that it is God, a distant and invisible being, who is present and at work beneath the forms of everyday life. Alternatively, one may settle for the unseen but palpable presences of angels and saints. However, the experience of the primitive does not stop at the boundaries of the sacred. The source of a potent but unseen presence may be anyone in the community who wishes one harm: the secret witch, the secretive and unhappy immigrant, the solitary neighbor, or even the critical colleague. If we are to understand the history of the Christian Church in the West, moreover, we will need to understand what it is like to live in a world where these presences are felt.

To understand, express, and even perhaps to control the experience of such presences and forces has long been the function of religious language. What is remarkable, it seems to me, is that the experiences of fantasies, hallucinations and dreams could be articulated not only in the language of the people but in the more formal and authorized language of the Church itself. Although it may now seem strange to us, there was indeed a time when rulers and politicians, as well as sages and prophets, considered the dream and the unconscious to be a more or less important source of authority and direction. Roman civilization in the fourth century, for instance, and the Carolingian period in the eighth century allowed the discussion of dreams to take place not only in monasteries and temples but on the floor of the Senate or in the court of the king himself.[3] Those seeking to gratify the vanity of a senator or general could claim to have dreamed of his advancement to higher office, while those seeking to warn or admonish a ruler for maltreating the faithful or for brutalizing his people could report having seen the erring king suffering for his crimes in a hell populated by bestial and by angelic or demonic figures with a talent for unending torture. Indeed, some of the more ancient 'tours of hell' analyzed by Himmelfarb found angels performing some of the same functions as worms and beasts.[4]

However, public discourse over dreams was not always political. Healing cults, both pagan and Christian, used the dream not only to diagnose the illness or torment of a sufferer but also to imagine or pronounce a cure. As Patricia Cox Miller puts it of late Roman antiquity, '... faith in the therapeutic effect of the dream on unruly feelings was part of a culture pattern that persisted through quite different changes of social and religious landscape.'[5] This is a long way from the contemporary understanding of dreams as symptomatic of incestuous or murderous desires or expressive of harsh internal judgements for imaginary crimes.

It was not only pagans in trouble and in need of therapeutic assistance who were encouraged to dream. Christian ascetics also dreamed of the transformation of the bodies of those whom they had deeply loved but who had died, and in their dreams their grief was transformed into ecstatic reunion or triumphs over time. For some of these ascetics, dreams were more real than life itself; they '... could reflect an autobiographical "I" that was distanced from the "I" of messy historical entanglements.'[6] Indeed, one ascetic whom Miller has studied saw his dreams as being reality itself. Thus he was literally an answer to his mother's prayer, and in one of his mother's dreams he actually healed her of an illness.[7] In his own dreams, moreover, he encountered and experienced a heaven-on-earth that he considered to be truly divine, as opposed to his mundane life as a bishop. This ascetic was Gregory Nazianzen, and as a bishop of Constantinople in the fourth century he was thus in a position to publicize his dreams, which he forthrightly did. Thus in the world in which Christian thought was framed, dreams and the unconscious were part of the public, and not merely private world. Notably, the way to a sacred truth that superseded common knowledge was through the depths of the soul perceived through dreams.

Thus the sacred provides a model of the primitive: one that is idealized, or sanitized, and thereby reduced to imaginable and manageable proportions. The world of animal or bestial passions becomes a gargoyle or, even more idealized, a figure of radiant though as yet bodily beauty. Take, for example, another fourth-century Christian ascetic in the Roman empire, Gregory of Nyssa, who saw in his dreams a figure of his dead sister. In his dream, writes Patricia Cox Miller, his sister's body had been radiant with a holy beauty, transfigured beyond anything that might have been sullied by physical passion or destroyed by death.[8] Even in her lifetime, Miller notes, Gregory had seen his sister in these transfigured, angelic images. As we might say, he had idolized her. Gregory had a horror of the physical, of the life of the body, and considered it bestial. No wonder that his love for his departed sister was expressed in his dream somewhat indirectly as white light streaming from her dead body. Thus in his dreams Gregory finds symbols for his physical passions: idols that imitate and yet overcome them and even make them sublime.

To incorporate, in however sublime or disguised a form, an affection or affiliation that has otherwise been excluded from a society or from an individual's consciousness is the task of the sacred. No wonder, then, that the Christian ascetics like Gregory of Nyssa dreamed of the dead, whom they had adored, as being radiant and nearly divine. Note also that they called such dream-images *eidola*. They are, as I have just suggested, idols of the soul, since they represent possibilities too dangerous to admit into the conscious precincts of the psyche in their natural form. Disguised as idols, however, these images allowed the mystic to recover a sense of life in the body that was otherwise despised and rejected.

However, even in late antiquity, individuals were not left entirely to their own devices to make sense of these nocturnal images. Patricia Cox Miller has found in the discourse of Stoics and Platonists, as well as in the records of the many temples devoted to healing under the auspices of Asclepius and of gods such as Isis and Osiris, ample evidence that the tours of the unconscious were even then guided by experts in the topography of that psychic terrain.[9] There were practitioners and temples, images and texts that gave structure and meaning to personal fantasies and visions. The point, however, is that the language of the unconscious was widely shared and intimately understood not only by experts but by the many who came to them for help. As Patricia Cox Miller puts it:

> In Stoic theory, dreams allow the soul to stand outside its immersion in the everyday and to reflect on its course in a broader context, conceived theologically as a cosmic structure undergirded by the gods. Divination by dreams was geared toward such imaginative shaping of individuals' subjectivity. Without this recognition, it can only be seen as a mechanical technique, not as the lived practice that it was.[10]

In these passages we can find Miller going to some length to demystify the demon, to see behind mythology various individual and communal capacities to find meaning in circumstance and hope in the middle of suffering and trial.

In dreams, societies have long sought to find the sources of hitherto unimaginable sedition or enlightenment, destruction or redemption. As a lived practice, therefore, the interpretation of dreams was undertaken with the help of demons who could enlarge the individual's sense of both the dangers and possibilities of everyday life. It is as if the demon was the mediator of the environment to the individual: a source of perspective and guidance that '... avoids being overwhelmed by circumstance and looks instead for patterns of meaning, however somber their figurations may be ... daemons appear to be those factors that enlarge the sphere of the merely personal by putting it in touch – "ghosting" it – with the collective wisdom of the human community.'[11]

However, I am skeptical of some of these antique claims to spirituality put forward under the name of dreams. To a modern, aware that dreams express aspects of the self that have been suppressed or split off from ordinary consciousness, it is not surprising to find in the dreams of these early ascetics something quite primitive: passions that are clearly erotic; Oedipal triumphs over rivals to parental affection, and a glorified sense of the self that gives narcissism a bad name. It is also not surprising to find, beneath these layers of imaginary triumph, a diminished sense of self. That, too, is primitive.

My own skepticism, however, is compatible with the doubts of these early dreamers themselves. The theologies of mystics indeed varied in their willingness to take literally the images of dreams as facts about themselves, and some were particularly aware that these images were colored with the various hues of passion. There was something primitive, or at least primal, in the thinly disguised triumphs and longings of the mystical dream. No wonder that the ascetics themselves, however, were skeptical of whether or not they lived up to the more fanciful self-images of their dreams.[12]

As this brief excursion into a discussion of fourth-century dreaming suggests, the capacity of language to evoke the landscape of the psyche is not modern at all; it is classical and antique. It is also clear that the language of classical and late antiquity had ways not only of talking about this terrain but of interpreting it through the study of dreams and of personifying it in beings such as angels or demons. It is these spirits, at once both foreign and domestic, and both internal to the soul, who stand for the capacity of the individual to sense the full range of possibility in the social and natural environments, from enmity and disease to illicit love and impermissible objects of desire. Dreams seemed to embody a possibility that had been excluded from the world that claimed to have a monopoly on reality. In psychoanalytic terms, this insistence on something other than the reality-principle functioned as a warning of dangers or as a promise of possibilities for satisfaction that the world as then constructed could not give. Dreams and fantasies were potentially subversive.

To control the interpretation of dreams would therefore have been essential for any institution or professional group that sought to shape the imagination of a people and to keep human aspiration within a range of legitimate and possible satisfaction. To theologians like Gregory of Nyssa, as Miller observes, the capacity of the ordinary individual to have and to interpret meaningful dreams was undeniable, and yet it seemed to Gregory that such interpretations encroached on the capacity of God to choose certain extraordinary dreamers as vehicles for divine revelation.[13] Indeed, 'He seems at once enticed by and wary of the dreamy *eidola* that haunt the soul ... but others in late antiquity, among polytheists as well as in his own monotheistic tradition, were more willing to give such constructs a place in processes of ordinary human understanding.'[14] Thus Stoics would tend to see dreams not only as indications of their fate but as a source of insight into the meaning of frustration and tragedy, while healers might evoke the auspices of Asclepius in temples that offered sanctuary and therapy for the diseased and depressed.

What is at stake in these theological as well as anthropological or historical discussions is possession of the psychological images, the *eidola* that represent the soul to itself.[15] It is no wonder, then, that Gregory insists on the need for divinely inspired practitioners, like Joseph in the biblical narrative, to interpret the dreams of more ordinary mortals. Consider, for instance, what would happen if individuals were being licensed to divine things for themselves; each, like Freud, would be his or her own priest and might claim the authority to interpret not only dreams but also Scripture itself. No wonder that Freud compared himself favorably to the biblical Joseph who interpreted the dreams of the Pharaoh.

We are still, even in Miller's own analysis, a long way from the understanding offered by Freud that the demons of the imagination, and the capacity to interpret them, inhere in the soul itself, and that one can teach oneself how to see in dreams the projections of one's own longings or one's own unwanted desires. Even Miller herself, intent as she is on de-mystifying the cultural imagination of late antiquity, does not ascribe to individuals the authority or the capacity to transcend their own circumstances and to sense the world in which they are living on their own terms. At best, as she notes, dreams – interpreted by the individual – give them access to 'the collective wisdom of the human community.'[16] Granted that dreams 'function as sources of self-awareness and ethical reflection,' they are still 'a daemonic production,' and for the historian or anthropologist they are signs of a collective imagination.[17] As Miller later puts it, '... it is clear that faith in the therapeutic effect of the dream on unruly feelings was part of a culture pattern that persisted through quite different changes of social and religious landscape.'[18]

However, it seems to me to be a mistake to set up a hypothetical view of late antiquity as being psychologically naïve in order to dramatize an alleged difference from modernity. Not everyone lived in a universe enchanted by demons or confused their waking state with dreaming. Even those who cultivated these borderline states of consciousness were not without their own critical faculties. Were figures, like Gregory of Nyssa or Gregory of Nazianzen in the fourth century CE, so unable to recognize their own cravings and fears in the images, the *eidola*, of their dreams? After all, in dreaming of his dead brother as though the brother had returned to life and scored his own victory over death, Gregory of Nazianzen sensed that he was picturing his brother 'by my desire, if not by the very truth.'[19] Maybe Gregory himself knew that his image of a dead brother now alive once again and now seen as forever free from the chains of death was merely an idol of his own imagination.

To grasp what Gregory (Nazianzen) meant and understood, as well as to sense what was beyond his imagination, we need to understand the scope and power of religious language.[20] I have been suggesting that religious language is capable of embodying the excluded possibility. In a very literal sense, Gregory's language, as he interprets his own dream, embodies the possibility that a dead person, indeed a very dear brother, has returned. The dead live; the absent are present. For Gregory, furthermore, the body itself was a possibility to be excluded: a dead weight even in one's lifetime that held one back from fully understanding and envisioning the purity of God. It was the source not only of limitations but also of passions that blinded one to the divine vision.

In his dreams, therefore, as in his theological interpretation of his dream, Gregory's language itself incorporates the body in its glorified state: victorious over death and decay and transcending even the passage of time itself. After all, his description of his brother came during Gregory's funeral oration for him in which he elaborated on his dream and evoked 'the return of the rejected body as sign': rejected because it was fallen, rejected because it was physical and therefore riddled with sinful design and passion.[21] Indeed, for Gregory, the idealized vision of his brother's glorified body was not merely a dream but a sign of the reality of a new humanity in which the purity of the image of God in the original Adam had been restored. The very possibility for living purely in the presence of God, a possibility once excluded by original sin, was now incorporated into signs, the *eidola*, of the dream and into Gregory's oration in which he announced his brother's return.[22]

To a modern, or at least to one who understands images of this sort as projections of the unconscious and its wishes or fears, these *eidola* are merely idols: personifications of the human desire to transcend time and death itself. They may be glorified images of someone whose death is grievous; they may be equally glorified images of a mythic figure like Adam. They may be images of a body that is larger than life. In any event, in psychoanalytic terms they are mere projections of a wish to recover someone who is lost, of a wish also to transcend death, and of a fear of the final extinction of the self. Gregory appears to have wondered if these images were merely the projections of his desire: not the cure for such longings but a symptom of them. However, if Miller is to be followed, he lacked the sense of an inner, substantial self that would have enabled him to recognize these images as mere wish fulfillment and to fall back on his own spiritual resources. He is an alien to himself: alien because still in his own body: 'I emphasize the dreams' role in reformulating the identity of the *dreamer* ... They picture in imaginal terms what Gregory is *not* but deeply desires to be: no longer in exile' (emphasis in original).[23] To be in exile, to be an alien, is to be estranged from oneself, and the cure requires the restoration of a purity of selfhood lost in the original Adam.

Later we will explore Freud's own attempt to come to terms with the death of someone who was like a brother to him. In his intense, loving and ambivalent affection, Freud located many of his own fantasies, and in his grief Freud encountered his own difficulties with irrevocable loss and with the passage of time. If religious language has its origins in the attempt to incorporate the possibility excluded by death, the possibility for a return of the one who was so deeply – if ambivalently – loved, psychoanalytic language has its origins in the attempt once and for all to cut those losses and to recognize in the images of the departed aspects of one's own soul in psychological exile. However, I am getting ahead of the story with this brief excursion into the present. Let us return to the world of the fourth century and to the attempt of religious language literally to do the impossible.

To understand the worlds of the two Gregorys, one of Nyssa, the other of Nazianzen, we have to imagine what it is like to feel that time is itself a mortal insult to one's own soul, to one's very being. In this connection Miller speaks of the imagined 'fall of human beings into time.'[24] Life was lived, then, in a form of anticipatory grief. It is for them as if being-in-time were a contradiction in terms. Theologically put, this meant that the Fall, Adam's sin, was what subjected individuals to the passage of time and hence to death itself. The self was at best insubstantial and empty as it lived in the exile of time: its true identity hidden in a realm of divine images that could only be revealed to those with the insight of the saint or through dreams. The knowledge of death thus retroactively deprived the self of moment.

If life lived in time and under the threat of death could deprive the self of significance, perhaps through self-renunciation and ascetic practice the individual could turn the tables on death and the passage of time. As we have seen, Gregory of Nyssa had doubts about the value of dreams, but his own dreams gave him the courage of his religious convictions about the importance of an ascetic renunciation of this world and of the attempt to empty the soul in this life that it might be filled with a more divine substance. If he fed his soul on these dreamy images, these *eidolas*, of a redeemed and transformed body, he might fill the emptiness created by his ascetic discipline of renouncing every wish, every passion, every longing that was tainted by the passage of time, that is by life itself. Certainly he knew a lot about dream images, *eidola* and the life of perennial grief. In fact, like Gregory Nazianzen, he mourned the death of someone very dear, in his case a sister, Macrina, and had a revelatory dream, not directly about his sister but about the bones of the martyrs. As Miller puts it, 'Like Gregory of Nazianzen's dreams of his brother, Gregory of Nyssa's dream of his sister allowed him to see through a dead body to a body that was lively in another register … a shimmering object that mediated the gap between the paradigmatic worlds of Adam and the resurrection …'[25] Indeed, this image of a body and soul somewhere between this life and the next, applied to his sister Macrina even in her lifetime.

Again, to the modern reader, and especially to one with a psychoanalytic viewpoint, the ascetic attack on the psyche is not the cure but the disease. It accentuates a loss of self and makes it a virtue, a way of life, rather than treating it as an illness or a form of suffering to be overcome by finding something solid within. Worse yet, it is dreams of those whom one continues to love passionately after their death, especially when they are personified in images of a radiant and transformed selfhood, that make the self seem less than it truly is. Without these glorified, one might say grandiose, images of a self that transcends the passage of time, the inner self would be more readily available and acceptable, wounded and mortal though it is. I will return to these considerations in the next chapter as we begin to discuss Freud's modern search for what is original, basic and primitive about the human psyche. His asceticism is a far cry from that of the two fourth-century Gregorys we have considered in this chapter.

There is still reason, however, to encourage religious language to recover some of its forgotten possibilities through renewing its acquaintance with the unconscious. Very early in the development of Christian thought and practice, monastic asceticism was testing the limits of human possibility in closed communities and in the solitary devotions of monks in the desert. That is, these ascetics were seeking to go beyond both secular and sacred models of the possible to encounter ultimate possibility, that is, the Sacred itself. Speaking of the formative work of John Cassian, an Eastern monk who became the teacher of Western monastics and whose work underlay much of the later Rule of St. Benedict, Columba Stewart writes:

Anything that distracts from the monastic goal is subversive: obsessions, vices, secular involvements undertaken for unholy purposes. Mental images that limit one's encounter with the divine are subversive, such as pagan idols or the well intended but equally dangerous piety he attributes to the Anthropomorphites. A monk needs matter for prayer that neither distracts or subverts and that furthers progress toward the goal.[26]

The ascetic goal, of course, was to achieve purity of heart by willing one thing: absolute reliance on the presence of God. To put it in less devotional terms, it was to expose the soul to ultimate possibility by eliminating all the lesser forms of the Sacred and by avoiding any thought or impulse that would shield the soul from the radical uncertainty of the presence of God. The exercise of the ascetic, then, was to forge the soul through exposing the individual to what alone matters most both in life and in death, with no guarantees of achieving an awareness of the divine presence, with few guidelines for practice, and with the awareness of awful penalties for failure, that is, the death of the soul itself.

In these respects, of course, ascetic practice was very much like modern psychoanalysis. There is the same impatience with distraction and with superficial levels of the imagination. The two share an insistence on going deeper into the psyche, where words fail and only inchoate images and longings give clues to the presence of the innermost self. In both there is a radical uncertainty about achieving the goal of a full apprehension of the soul. Like Cassian, Freud was realistic about resistance and the desire to avoid passions that were painful because they were impossible to fulfill. Cassian insisted not only on the importance of sexual passion but on the difficulty of ever reaching beyond it to a less turbulent and demanding level of the soul. Here, as Columba Stewart notes of Cassian, he avoided any 'Pelagian overoptimism about ascetical possibility' while nonetheless staying focussed on the goals of preserving the soul from becoming satisfied or entranced by anything less than the Sacred. Nothing less than pure, ultimate possibility could save the soul from premature death, and yet such radical openness to uncertainty could hardly be expected of those who seek some satisfaction in the more immediate worlds of face to face adoration and affection.[27] Here is Stewart again:

> Cassian founds his teaching about chastity on the eschatological assumptions that still remain the theological basis for monastic celibacy. His starting point, as always, was a conviction that the true homeland of believers lies beyond the horizons of this world. The longing for that homeland where humankind will be free from the constraints of mortality, and turn unhesitatingly to the infinite vistas of the glory of God, inspired monks to their otherwise inexplicable renunciations.

The encounter with ultimate possibility requires what psychoanalysts call the uprooting of emotion-laded images in the mind, or cathexes with particular people and places, events and memories. It requires that one transcend old loves that live on in the timeless world of the libido, if individuals are to seek the eternity of God. To replace a spurious eternity in the soul, where loves do not die, with the real eternity in which the soul itself will not die, is at the heart of ascetic practice, whereas the psychoanalyst can offer only the provisional hope that the soul will be discovered or will emerge before it dies.

I do not mean for a moment to suggest equivalence between fourth-century asceticism and twentieth-century psychoanalysis. From a psychoanalytic viewpoint, the monastic preoccupation with chastity and the overcoming of secular desire would be a symptom of the disease, not the cure. That is because the monastic preoccupation with chastity assured that exquisite attention would be paid to the erotic stirrings of the psyche. Whether it was the mere sight of a woman's face, the memory of earlier sexual experience, or the prospect of prohibited sexual ecstasies, the monastic psyche was trained to focus on erotic fantasy: the very staples of ancient descents into hell. From an analytic viewpoint, this allows the repressed material to continue to return; the excluded possibility is embodied once again in the very discipline that removed it from the realm of realistic aspiration.

Religious language, then, in embodying the excluded possibility, is very much like what psychoanalysis calls a reaction formation. The psyche's very defense against sexual desire reinforces and perpetuates itself. Like a patient engaged in an interminable analysis, the monk remains constantly vigilant for the return of repressed sexual wishes. In the name of putting such desire behind him, the monk thus holds open the door to the past. The descent into the hell of the psyche becomes a lifetime journey.

There is a limit, then, in the extent to which one can draw analogies between psychoanalytic and early Christian asceticism. Granted that, as Stewart puts it, '... the ascetical struggle extended into the realm of sleep and the unconscious, where only God could bring peace.' Both Cassian, the fourth-century monk, and Freud, the twentieth-century analyst, indeed paid very close attention to dreams as doors into the unconscious and sought a practice that would resolve, once and for all, unconscious struggles. Granted also that the monastic discipline looked forward to a time when, for the monk, even the sight of nakedness would be no more stimulating and disturbing than any other vision. Granted that for both Freud and Cassian there was a role for the will in resolving unconscious wishes and conflicts, nonetheless, as the above quotation suggests, for Cassian the final arbiter of the unconscious is God.

For Freud, on the other hand, the longing for a fatherly figure who will lead us out of temptation may last a lifetime, but it is not the way out of the wilderness. Freud wanted his colleagues to grow up, abandon their homosexual longings for an omniscient father confessor, and to take their journey into their own hands. The struggle in the desert continues only so long as the will wishes it to continue. That is, for Freud, there is no point in being a journeyman all one's life. One can at last say goodbye to the longing to be an apprentice to some master whose superior skill and knowledge will rescue one from dependence and helplessness. One can arrive spiritually; one can actually call one's soul one's own. For Cassian, however, the way out of the ascetic desert is only through the agency of God; there must be divine rescue from the temptations of sexuality, since the will cannot in the end set one free.

Like Freud, then, the monk Cassian viewed the individual's dreams as diagnostic of the soul. Thus he played close attention to the dreams that issued in nocturnal emissions 'because they can indicate the progress of chastity in the life of the [male] monk. Only grace can cross the border between waking and sleeping, between conscious and unconscious states.'[28] This preference for a life of liminality that gave free play both to the soul and to the workings of divine grace was indeed a move away from the mundane. Religious language could now encompass more than a matter-of-fact listing of disciplines and requirements, of hours devoted to the this-and-that of monastic life. Indeed, religious language could embody the possibilities excluded from ordinary consciousness; the repressed could return. In the return of these excluded spiritual elements there was indeed an attempt to keep the soul itself from dying in a condition of repressed self-awareness. Those aspects of the psyche that were split off were being returned to consciousness; as Freud would later put it, where *id* was, there would *ego* be. But here the analogy between early monastic asceticism and psychoanalysis comes to an abrupt stop. The perennial journey of the Christian soul is not for the psychoanalyst or the modern analytic patient. They prefer and can achieve a descent into spiritual depths from which there is indeed a return. The bridge between conscious and unconscious states is traversed by introspection rather than by grace alone. The past is therefore not only open but can be fulfilled; chapters can be written in the life of the soul and portions of the book closed. There is an end in sight: an end to the perennial return of unfinished and unfulfilled passion and longing.

By way of contrast, the monastic excursion into the world of limitless possibility had created a spiritual descent into a world of endless probation and trial, except for the possible advent of a divine rescue that could never be guaranteed. The stage was set for a continuous descent into hell, as a place from which there could be no spiritual return except by divine intervention. Paradoxically, Cassian's limited assertion of the capacity of the will to open the way for grace to operate in the soul lays the groundwork for the notion of hell. That place of perpetual longing is one in which it is also too late to fulfill certain desires. They remain with undiminished intensity to consume the individual as though by an everlasting fire. There is no past or present in such a hell, only a despairing future of continued and endless suffering. It is a timeless world because there is no end to the suffering in sight: no divine rescue from sexual longing and desire. Perhaps that is why even the most ancient Greek 'tours of hell' often included, as Himmelfarb has noted, a river of fire: continuous, burning libidinal passion. No wonder that monastic asceticism tended to limit itself to hoping that such desire might, with sufficient grace, abate during one's lifetime.

We have seen how Cassian's assertion of the ascetic will kept open the necessity for divine grace to perform the final rescue of the soul from erotic desire. The more the soul pursued the presence of God, the more it found itself in need of divine assistance. On the other hand, the more the soul relied on the prospect of divine assistance, the more it was obligated to deploy the resources of the will to purify the soul of alternative desires. So long as the Church could keep the soul of the individual within the horns of this dilemma, so to speak, the less likely it would be that the soul would find its own sources of inspiration and authority. To put it another way, even Cassian's insistence on both the possibility and the necessity of divine grace placed severe limits on the capacity of the soul to heal itself of impossible longings while intensifying the responsibility of the individual for purifying the will of base intentions.

Here, then, is a second point at which the early Christian interest in dreams as signs of the soul's well-being diverges from any approach that would be compatible with modern psychoanalysis. The monastic preoccupation with sexual desire could become a repetitive and defensive maneuver that could well perpetuate sexual preoccupations. Now it is also clear that the monastic insistence on relying solely on the grace of God deprived the soul of its own capacity to heal itself, even though individuals were given increasing responsibility for their own salvation by Cassian's willingness to attribute to the individual some capacity for good will.

By inculcating a posture of continuous helplessness and reliance on divine grace and favor, Cassian made sure that individuals would be entirely responsible for their spiritual condition but would have no control over their own eventual salvation. Certainly the individual was deprived of control over the outcome of his or her efforts to purify the soul by Cassian's orthodox, Augustinian concern to preserve the freedom of God to dispose of individual salvation according to the divine will alone. Individuals were thus supposed to spend their lives in unceasing prayers in which they would plead for the assistance of God: a recipe for training the will into high levels of personal responsibility for an outcome over which the individual has no control. As I have suggested, these are the pre-conditions for a spiritual journey into the depths of hell.

However, even this slight intrusion of the human will on to the arena of divine grace was enough to alarm papal authority. In the sixth century, indeed, under Pope Celestine, there was a concerted effort to undo the damage done by Cassian's monastic teachings among the monks of Gaul. Stewart relates how two laymen in the region of Marseilles, early in the fifth century, complained to Augustine that some very well-known and well-placed saints were teaching a doctrine that accorded to individuals some measure of free will in matters of their own salvation: an offense against Augustinian views and, in the eyes of these laymen, a stance dangerously close to the heretical Pelagius.[29] Augustine's response came in 429–30, in the form of two essays on predestination and the perseverance of the saints, while a papal condemnation, couched in the most general of terms, followed soon afterward. Cassian's offense was his 'concurrence with the traditional eastern teaching that stirrings of good remain possible even to fallen mankind.'[30] For this allowance that 'some initiative, however feeble, of the human will' was still possible, Cassian's name entered the list of usual suspects in the councils of the church. Along with Origen and Evagrius, as Stewart puts it, Cassian believed

> that humans beings retained some vestige of their created goodness and can learn to walk again as God intended. He taught the necessity of grace, but it was a liberal grace pervading a creation still rich in possibility. In his view, monasticism, like the Christianity of which it is a trope, educates and develops the human person called forth by God from sin into freedom.[31]

There it is again: the suggestion that the Sacred, properly understood, is an environment of possibility that entails all that the human can hope for or dread – salvation and damnation. Into this environment the soul enters in some fear and trembling, no doubt, but enters knowing that he or she bears the responsibility for an outcome over which the individual still in the last analysis has no final control. In return for Cassian's willingness to threaten the idols of the Church with possibilities over which the Church itself had no final disposition, the Church suspected Cassian of being soft on the very heresy against which he was at some pains to argue, Pelagianism. We cannot here go into the nature of that heresy or its various protagonists, but the point is simple enough. Cassian's limited attempt to open the Church to the realm of the possible outside its domain was offensive and threatening to an institution that sought to monopolize all sources of inspiration and authority. For such an institution, the individual's own spiritual progress could only be seen as a return of the primitive self, untutored by institutional authority and practice.

If Cassian's own attempt to accord the will some control over its ultimate fate seems questionable by modern standards, it is because he schools the soul into a posture of helpless dependence on divine grace at the same time that he insists on probing the dreams of monks for access to those areas of the psyche that resist the will. Like Freud, he was a master of the study of resistance. Indeed he even thought that the progress of the will might reduce the effects of lust on the dreams of monks, especially those dreams that produced nocturnal emissions. Not only nature but one's 'inmost thoughts' could extend the life and force of sexual desire, and the monk was therefore obligated to examine his dreams for signs that the will had not yet perfected its control over the most private and unconscious sources of that desire.[32]

In his concentration on extending the domain of the rational part of the self and on the will, Cassian does resemble Freud. The two both seem to have subscribed to the Platonic notion that individuals are driven by destructive, angry emotions as well as by desire, and that both kinds of passion need to be brought under the control of the part of the self that surveys landscapes of possibility and makes decisions: Freud's ego, Plato's 'charioteer.'[33] Both also know that the soul can suffer a premature death if these emotions are not explored and understood in their native state, their natural condition, as that is revealed in the individual's dreams. Both understood that the sickness of the soul comes from avoiding intense emotion. Further, Cassian studied poignant sadness as well as exquisite moments of joy as states of the soul that marked stages along the way to spiritual completion. Tears, in particular, in both Cassian's view and in psychoanalytic practice, are often crucial signs of individual access to painful memory, but for Cassian they can also be tears of 'anticipation of future beatitude.'[34]

Even in this area of common ground between psychoanalysis and early monastic practice, however, the differences between the two are crucial. For Cassian it is possible for tears to continue, tears of sadness or compunction to continue throughout life.[35] The analysis of the soul is indeed interminable, because one is afraid of hell and faces the prospect of divine judgment.[36] Thus monks may be moved to tears by the prospect of hell, and they never outgrow the need to win divine approval: 'The monk progresses from fear to love and then to a "more sublime fear" lest the God who has loved or forgiven so much should be disappointed.'[37] Thus, as I have suggested earlier, the monastic discipline, for all its concern to avoid the death of the soul, keeps the soul in a state of perpetual adolescence: tantalized by possibility but afraid to make a decision that would finally relinquish the need for parental approval. One never arrives, and one never terminates the need for spiritual practice and correction under the guidance of a spiritual superior.

It would be a mistake to underestimate the role of hell in early Christian asceticism. Even Cassian's relatively benign discipline, with its emphasis on dreams and the role of the will in resolving primitive longings and desires, is like a descent into hell undertaken in order to avoid a final and irreversible descent into endless torment. The monk seeks to overcome and transcend the burning of sexual desire so that in the end he will not be destined to be tormented by hopeless desire in hell. In the same way the monk seeks in this life to suffer all the torments of a guilty soul so that he will not, after his death, suffer guilt when it is too late to make spiritual amends. Thus 'mindfulness of the past is necessary until God grants forgetfulness of sins and removes the "thorns of conscience from the inmost parts of the soul." '[38]

In psychoanalysis it is the individual who is responsible for creating the past: for putting behind one the torments of remorse and regret. That discipline also requires that one allow emotions to pass through the filter of choice and the will. One has a choice, then, as to whether or not to feel driven by sexual desire: a choice that concerns the very innermost thoughts and fantasies of the individual. In the two disciplines, as we have seen, there is a similar concern with allowing what has passed to become part of the past: a place where memory lives without intensity and regret or longing. Their difference is in the insistence of Christian asceticism on the individual's continued need for divine assistance and intervention. One never leaves home or arrives at a spiritual state in which one no longer needs to reach up and touch the guiding hand of the spiritual father or feel the presence or the absence of God.

In many ways, then, modern psychoanalysis picks up these strands of monastic discipline: a heightened sense of human possibility; realism about the persistence of unsatisfied and insatiable desire; a concern with the unconscious; an attempt to replace unconscious desires and fears with conscious reflection; an insistence on the soul's recovery through the experience of disturbing emotion that may have otherwise been split off from consciousness; an awareness that past emotional states continue to live within the soul and take on new life from fantasy and imagination as well as from the circumstances of the individual's social life; a concern with creating a past of memory and emotion that no longer haunts or determines the individual's present state of mind; an awareness that what is excluded from consciousness can indeed return and be embodied in physical and mental states; an awareness also that religious language, like the language of the dream, encodes these excluded possibilities. For Freud, however, hell is the continuation of desires and longings that are too late to fulfill, whereas for Cassian hell remains a future possibility, the fear of which is a necessary spur to spiritual progress.

The religious 'cure,' from a psychoanalytic viewpoint, is another form of the disease: a defense that perpetuates the threat for which it is intended to be the spiritual remedy. *The spiritual descent into hell thus becomes a perpetual journey because it is a projection of the past into the future.* Unfinished emotional states from the past are projected forward to a time when it is too late to complete or resolve them. From that place in the future they react back into the present as a mirror of the incomplete and longing soul: a reminder of the depths to which it is necessary yet to descend. In such a discipline the descent into hell can be an endless journey.

The soul may be lost for a variety of reasons. The soul may be lost because it is split off into a world from which it cannot emerge: its own hell, so to speak. The soul may be lost because it is partly dead and partly alive: in its own purgatory, as it were, where it seeks to recover itself by making up for lost time. The religious metaphors for the states of the soul remind us that something very fundamental is at stake here: the core of the self, and the source of the individual's inner sovereignty and vitality.

The spiritual dilemma of being condemned to take responsibility for spiritual states over which one has no final control escaped the confines of Christian asceticism and entered into a very popular literary mainstream. It is therefore to Dante that we turn in the next chapters. There we will find residues of the early monastic notion of a descent into hell and of early medieval dreams and visions of hell: the consequences of the compromise that we have been examining in this chapter between the resources and will of the individual, on the one hand, and the orthodox demand that the individual's rescue and salvation be left wholly to the determination of God. In Dante also we will find passions that are undying long after it is too late to fulfill them: too late not only because the individual is dead but because he or she is forever beyond the reach of divine grace. The language of the dream continues, and individuals still lack the capacity to put hopeless regret, remorse, hatred and desire in the past. Even the poet's descent into hell is a spiritual exercise that fails to create the past and keeps open the possibility of divine grace, heavenly ecstasies and a return to the beatitude of the infantile state. The language of the unconscious is still spoken, but the insights of psychoanalysis are still absent from the cure of souls.

## Notes

1 Eva Pocs (1999), *Between the Living and the Dead*, Budapest: Central European Press, p. 51.
2 This argument is treated at length through Ernesto DeMartino (1988), *Primitive Magic, The Psychic Powers of Shamans and Sorcerers*, Dorset, England: Prism Press.
3 Patricia Cox Miller (1994), *Dreams in Late Antiquity. Studies in the Imagination of a Culture*, Princeton NJ: Princeton University Press; Paul Edward Dutton (1994), *The Politics of Dreaming in the Carolingian Empire*, Lincoln and London: University of Nebraska Press.
4 Martha Himmelfarb (1983), *Tours of Hell. An Apocalyptic Form in Jewish and Christian Literature*, Philadelphia: The University of Pennsylvania Press, p. 121.
5 Cox Miller, op. cit., p. 109.
6 Ibid., p. 245.
7 Ibid., pp. 244–5.
8 Ibid., pp. 236 ff.
9 Ibid., pp. 54–5.
10 Ibid., 106 ff.
11 Ibid., pp. 56–7.

12 Ibid., p. 243.
13 Ibid., pp. 47 ff.
14 Ibid., p. 51.
15 As I have noted, Miller uses the term *eidola* in this context because Gregory of Nyssa does so himself.
16 Cox Miller, op. cit., p. 57.
17 Ibid., p. 59.
18 Ibid., p. 109.
19 Gregory of Nyssa, *Orationes 7.21, Patrologia Graeca*, J. P. Migne (ed.) (1857–66), translated in *A Select Library of Nicene and Post-Nicene Fathers*, Paris, 2nd Series, New York: Christian Literature Company, 1887–1902; quoted in Cox Miller, op. cit., p. 232.
20 In this discussion I am relying on Cox Miller, ibid., pp. 232 ff.
21 Ibid., p. 235.
22 Ibid., p. 235.
23 Ibid., p. 236.
24 Ibid., p. 238.
25 Ibid., pp. 237–8.
26 Columba Stewart (1998), *Cassius the Monk*, New York, Oxford: Oxford University Press, p. 110.
27 Ibid., p. 71.
28 Ibid., p. 77.
29 Ibid., pp. 20–21.
30 Ibid., p. 21.
31 Ibid., p. 22.
32 Ibid., p. 64.
33 Ibid., p. 64.
34 Ibid., p. 129.
35 Ibid., p. 129.
36 Ibid., p. 128.
37 Ibid., p. 129.
38 Ibid., p. 129.

# Chapter 6

# Overcoming the Primitive Self: Perennial Spiritual Journeys

The notion that there is an internal split within the psyche is very old indeed. The conflict, as St. Paul put it, is between the old man and the new man. The psychoanalyst Chasseguet-Smirgel speaks of a universal tendency toward perversion: toward a regression to a pre-oedipal stage of psychological development in which the child is hostile to any distinction between the genders or generations and rejects the limitations and requirements represented by the father.[1] It is the child or adolescent, clearly, that engages in a Faustian quest for more time and who likes to keep all his possibilities open; only the adult knows that these strivings mask a desire to have the original maternal landscape to oneself and that one cannot make up for lost time.

Longings for an earlier self may lead to chronic and unremitting spiritual antagonism within the psyche, namely between earlier and later selves. To resolve such an impasse requires what is in literary terms a descent into hell, where old rivalry, grandiosity and passion survive that, however they may be regretted, have not yet been relinquished or renounced. Take, for example, Dante's encounter with one soul in Hell. This unhappy shade had been a servant of Frederick II, but had been accused of treason and had been exiled from the court. The shade claims to Dante that he had been the envy of others for his privileged position as an advisor of the emperor and that their envy and scorn had caused him much suffering. Thus his own suicide was due to his thought that 'Dying would be a way to escape disdain,/making me treat my juster self unjustly,' (Canto XIII.66–68).[2] Unable to have more time, it being too late in Hell even at the last day for the suicidal soul to be reunited with his body except in the most bizarre and tragic fashion, he begs Dante to 'comfort my memory//Still prostrate from the blow that envy gave,' (Canto XIII.72–73).[3] It is as if the memory of someone is like his shadow or spiritual substance.

There is more than the usual anguish here for Dante, who is unable to ask the shade any questions 'because of pity that fills my heart': a clear violation of Virgil's earlier injunction to waste no pity on the fools of Hell. But it is among the self-destructive that Dante finds himself at a loss for words. Inevitably he asks Virgil further to interrogate the shade. Dante (Canto XIII.83) recounts Virgil's promise to the shade that, if that unhappy suicide will tell Dante how 'the soul is bound in knots like these,' the poet will 'make amends by freshening your fame/When he returns again to the world above,' (Canto XIII.49–50; Pinsky 1994:105,103).[4] Indeed the Canto itself becomes the promised memorial.

Thus the suicidal soul in hell is still engaged in this internal quarrel. While his self-destructive psyche lives on, his 'juster self' pleads that his memory be comforted by a poet who can tell the truth about him and thus revise his reputation: a breach, so to speak, in the contract with hell where it is always too late to find such comfort. It is as if Dante slips for a moment from Hell to Purgatory, where the dead implore him to remember their suffering and to comfort their memory. Hell is the only place where the past cannot be revised through constructive memory and where one's character, therefore, remains eternally fixed.

One can hardly miss the self-destructive tendency in this quarrel with one's more primitive self, in which the adult self consigns the remnants of the younger self to continual torment. Remember Nietzsche's comment: 'the young soul, tortured by all kinds of disappointments, finally turns suspiciously against itself, still hot and wild, even in its suspicion and pangs of conscience – how wroth it is with itself now!' *It is as if the self-destructive soul feeds on its former self to nourish its self-hatred, whereas the soul who is able to accept its being-in-time allows the past, as it were, to disappear into the mist and can be forgotten.*

There are various sorts of metaphors for the antagonism between the more primitive and more developed self. St. Paul, as we have noted, referred to the old man at war with the new, and he argued that one must put away 'childish things.' Even for Paul, however, it was not possible simply to let the past slip away into forgetfulness. On the contrary, he explored in complex metaphoric detail the relation of the 'old' Israel to the 'new.' Remember also Dante's notion that Florence was locked into a conflict between its earlier self, dedicated to Mars, and its later identity, when it was devoted to John the Baptist. Its later, 'juster self' remained in conflict with the remnants of the earlier, warlike elements of the city embodied in the remnants of a statue of Mars. Thus the pacific and the martial, the later and the earlier developments of the self, continued in a death agony of recurring conflict. As Goethe puts it through Faust:

> Two souls, alas! reside within my breast
> and each is eager for a separation:
> in throes of coarse desire, one grips
> the earth with all its senses;
> the other struggles from the dust
> to rise to high ancestral spheres.[5]

I, ll.1112–1117

Here, of course, the metaphor distinguishes a more primitive from a higher self, but the conflict can easily be transposed into a war between one's more youthful and animal spirits and one's mature, even celestial destiny. In fact, Goethe starts Faust's journey toward hell by contrasting Faust's longing for the Infinite with various exemplars of animal spirits: revelers in a bar behaving piggishly, and apes being all too human (I, ll.2075 ff., 2337 ff.).[6] As Mephistopheles puts it: 'self-contradiction, when complete, is to the wise/ as much a mystery as to the fool' (I, ll.2558–59).[7] It is the primitive self, the excluded spiritual possibility, that comes back to haunt the self not yet reconciled to the costs of maturity.

The search for his more primitive self causes Faust to return to the polymorphous, even perverse sexuality of youth. Faust, staring into a magic mirror, becomes entranced by the vision he sees there of a woman beautiful beyond description (I, ll.2429 ff.).[8] In addition to seeking to recover his animal spirits, which had given him a youthful buoyancy, Faust looks for his androgynous self and is saved only when the sound of angels reminds him of what Mephistopheles calls the 'discordant, nasty tinklings' of 'juvenile-androgynous bumbling' (I, 11. ll.685–688).[9] It is as if, ignoring the boundaries of gender and time, he can continue the search for limitless joy: for 'the bliss all hearts desire,' (I, 11. ll.729–30).[10]

What Goethe takes for the cure, of course, is therefore a symptom of the original disease that makes the individual impatient with limits and with the passage of time. The attempt to recover excluded possibility may doom the psyche to erotic longings that will never be satisfied, while reinforcing tendencies to wait for rescue at the hands of angels. Thus here in literary form we have the same dilemma posed by earlier Christian asceticism: an intensified sense of personal responsibility for overcoming sexual longings and the necessity of waiting for divine intervention. This dilemma, however, has long since escaped the confines of the monastic community and has become endemic, so to speak, in the literary tradition. The return of the primitive under Christian auspices that had so interested Freud may well have been brought home to him through his reading of Goethe. The angels that come finally to transport Faust's soul thus sound a note that Freud echoed: 'what hurts your inward self/you must reject it,' (I, 11. ll.747–48).[11] The secular descent into hell does require one to experience the infantile self, but it seeks a way out of the adult's agonized struggle with the past. There is a parting of the ways, then, between the romantic and the psychoanalytic descents into hell. Whereas the angels would transport Faust's soul to a cherubic and 'androgynous' heaven, the secular descent requires a final renunciation of the milieu of infancy: a willingness to let the infantile self become evanescent and eventually perish.

The milieu of infancy includes the dyad in which the child and mother are united without the child's having had to endure the long process of maturing.

This primitive self is opposed by a later stage of development in which the individual is all too anxious to prove himself or herself and to earn rewards legitimately. Even the neurotic, however, is driven by the hope of a triumphant and exclusive access to the mother. Thus the earlier self competes with the later one, which in turn judges the earlier self rather harshly: all the more severely, of course, because the later self is also tempted to regress to the illusions of omnipotence and equality of the pre-oedipal child.

One side of the psyche thus seeks to live in a world without limitations and invidious distinctions, in which all souls are mixed and matched in fluid and fantastic fashion; this side is at war with a later stage of the self, which abhors such perversity and seeks to meet the temporal demands of everyday life. Conversely, the later stage, the obsessional or neurotic, draws its reason for being from its conflict with the earlier, more perverse and playful stage of development. To put it another way, if the earlier stage is narcissistic in its sense of its own imaginary powers, the later stage is masochistic; it is necessary to suffer, so to speak, on the way to glory, if one is to earn one's eternal rewards.[12]

Thus is set in motion a perennial contest within the psyche, on which one side is sustained by passions that refuse to die, while the other side professes to know that it is already too late for those passions to be satisfied. The psyche at war with itself undergoes a continual struggle against opposing tendencies: the poet versus the pilgrim, the dreamer versus the realist, the apprentice and journeyman versus the master and professional. Eventually the dreams of eventual glory may go underground, so that even the relatively more neurotic than perverse, the pilgrim and the professional and not only the poet and dreamer, are sustained by a vision of timeless union with the original matrix. Never mind that they profess to be wholly engaged in the demands of a world in which time is always running out.

Once it has become entrenched, of course, the earlier stage of development dies very hard indeed. Under pressure from the later, more obsessional self, the earlier self may go undergound, become repressed altogether, or even split off entirely from consciousness; there it begins to die and is therefore always running out of time. The attack of the obsessional self on the earlier narcissistic and perverse self becomes a holy war under certain religious auspices, which requires the death of the earlier self and a strict adherence to the law, to the principle of the division of the genders, and to social authority. Even Chasseguet-Smirgel herself contrasts the perverted psychological universe to the 'Biblical universe:' biblical because it emphasizes distinctions between genders and generations and because it places strict limitations on the expression of desire. Thus the requirement to punish the self for its early lack of maturity seems to be endemic within Western religious culture and continues to be the source of conflict and schism in many Protestant denominations.

Here, as a voice that is typically associated with a secular modernity, is Nietzsche's version of the perspective of someone who perpetuates the quarrel between the old man and the new:

> The wrathful and reverent attitudes characteristic of youth do not seem to permit themselves any rest until they have forged men and things in such a way that these attitudes may be vented on them ... Later, when the young soul, tortured by all kinds of disappointments, finally turns suspiciously against itself, still hot and wild, even in its suspicion and pangs of conscience – how wroth it is with itself now! ... how it takes revenge for its long self-delusion, just as if it had been a deliberate blindness! In this transition one punishes oneself with mistrust against one's own feelings; one tortures one's own enthusiasm with doubts; indeed, one experiences even a good conscience as a danger ...[13]

Nietzsche knows of a continuous and extensive punishment of the self for its earlier, less mature stage of development. Old disappointments and struggles are perpetuated rather than finished. Indeed, Nietzsche goes on to say that 'Ten years later one comprehends that all this, too – was still youth.'[14]

This project of retrospective self-condemnation and continuous self-doubt has far more in common with self-hatred than with a secular descent into hell. It is as if one cannot go from one stage in life to the next without holding on to rejected aspects of the former self rather than simply consigning them to the past without remorse and regret. Freud, as we will see, is no stranger to this tendency, but he locates it in his unconscious, analyzes it in his dreams, and seeks thereby to move beyond repetitive self-punishment.

To descend into the unconscious is a necessary step toward the recovery of the soul. Certainly such a descent is necessary if one is to recover suppressed or moribund parts of the psyche. These parts of the soul may have been lost because someone, deeply loved, had died, or because these aspects of the psyche could not thrive in a 'civilized' society. Perhaps they were too primitive, whether because they were too grandiose, or jealous, or vindictive, or because they were too passive and filled with hopeless longing. To recover the psyche, however, requires just such a journey back to one's earlier self, if only to part with it while keeping a few mementos of one's youth.

Ultimately, to recover the psyche it is necessary to terminate one's love affairs with the dead. For Freud the dead represented both his longing for timeless relationships and his unconscious, murderous fantasies. On the one hand, the dead come back in his dreams (as 'revenants') because of his fond memories of them or because he continued to use them as a disguise for his more hateful emotions. The ghosts of his former colleagues and rivals were 'late' not only because they were dead, and not simply because he had eliminated them psychologically in his wish to have the field to himself. These ghosts were also late because they were deadened aspects of his own psyche. The dead thus came back to him in his dreams because they represented split-off and repressed aspects of himself from earlier stages of his development when he was impatient with anyone who stood in his way toward higher status, authority and recognition.

Let us now turn to the dream that Freud reported, in which he is visited by some of the figures from his past at the Vienna Institute. In *The Interpretation of Dreams* he describes what he calls a 'fine specimen' of a dream:

> I had gone to Brucke's laboratory at night, and, in response to a gentle knock on the door, I opened it to (*the late*) Professor Fleischl, who came in with a number of strangers and, after exchanging a few words, sat down at his table. This was followed by a second dream. My friend Fl. [Fliess] had come to Vienna unobtrusively in July. I met him in the street in conversation with my (*deceased*) friend P., and went with them to some place where they sat opposite each other as though they were at a small table. I sat in front of its narrow end. Fl. spoke about his sister and said that in three quarters of an hour she was dead, and added some such words as 'that was the threshold.' As P. failed to understand him, Fl. turned to me and asked me how much I had told P. about his affairs. Whereupon, overcome by strange emotions, I tried to explain to Fl. that P. (could not understand anything at all because he) was not alive. But what I actually said – And I myself noticed the mistake – was '**Non vixit**.' I then gave P. a piercing look. Under my gaze he turned pale; his form grew indistinct and his eyes a sickly blue – and finally he melted away. I was highly delighted at this and I now realized that Ernest Fleischl, too, had been no more than an apparition, a 'revenant' ['ghost' – literally, 'one who returns']; and it seemed to me quite possible that people of that kind only existed as long as one liked or could be got rid of if someone wished it. [emphasis added][15]

Freud's journey into the primitive levels of his own psyche unearths the memory of a profoundly embarrassing encounter in which it was he himself who had been emotionally annihilated when attacked for being late. On that painful occasion, the head of the Vienna Physiological Institute, Brucke, had confronted Freud and criticized him for being late to work; it was an encounter which Freud describes as devastating: 'What overwhelmed me were the terrible blue eyes with which he looked at me and by which I was reduced to nothing – just as P. was in the dream, where, to my relief, the roles were reversed.'[16] In that first encounter years earlier with Brucke at the Institute, it is Freud who is 'late' in both senses of the word; he is tardy but, being 'reduced to nothing,' he is also as good as dead. That is, he is mortified in the presence of this powerful other person. Thus in the dream he similarly mortified 'P' in a reversal of roles. As Freud recalls:

> This reproach for coming too late became the central point of the dream but was represented by a scene in which Brucke, the honored teacher of my student years, leveled this reproach at me with a terrible look from his blue eyes … The other

figure in the dream was allowed to keep the blue eyes ['P.'], but the annihilating role was allotted to me – a reversal which was obviously the work of wish-fulfillment.[17]

One does not have to be a psychoanalyst to see here the combination of longing and revolt that characterized, in Freud's view, the ties binding sons to fathers.

There is indeed a residue of very primitive, indeed magical, thinking in the psychological trick to which Freud is pointing when he says that, '… to my relief, the roles were reversed.' In the dream, then, it is Freud rather than his superior whose gaze is withering; it is his victim ('P.') who, like the superior, had blue eyes, but the victim's eyes are now a 'sickly blue.' Freud himself is coming back like a 'revenant' in this dream, but it is also his younger self who is returning with a vengeance: catching up with those who have gone before, notably his senior colleague in the guise of 'P.' This is the same younger self who had engaged in various psychological murders in order to have the field to himself.

It is not only Freud's younger and more viciously competitive self who is returning in this dream, however. Also making a comeback is a part of the self that had been paralyzed by too much emotion: the part that had disappeared in the presence of others who were overpoweringly attractive or frightening, or that was so mortified that one can properly speak of its temporary death. The sign of the psychic 'comeback' is that the will is no longer paralyzed; one can consign others to the past, just as in this dream Freud finally recognized that the others were merely 'apparitions' rather than real. Note, of course, that Freud is here describing a return of the primitive psyche's tendency to engage in child's play, to turn the tables, and by magical thinking to settle old scores. He was, as I have suggested, the source of his own insights into the patriarchal and fratricidal quarrels of the primitive horde.

There is no statute of limitations, however, on old trauma, especially when the trauma was intensified by a state of mind in which the individual's usual defenses and boundaries were breached, and the individual, either terrified or entranced, suffered at least a partial death of the psyche. When a person's memories are imbued with the helplessness, fascination and magical thinking of the child, it may be difficult, even impossible, to recover enough memory of the original event to allow a person in later years to experience once again that original loss, so as finally to consign it to the past. However, the past continues to haunt the present only so long as one wishes it to. People have the anxieties that they want to have, and they hold on to the attachments they want to keep, so long as they have unfinished emotional business with the objects of their hatred or desire. Thus the passed can be consigned to the 'past' only if one wills and wishes it to be.

A prime example of the ability to create the past through an act of the will is, as I have suggested, Freud himself. It is Freud who pitilessly confronts his past with analytical self-understanding and therefore with full knowledge that it is too late to undo his earlier 'crimes' or to prevent the death of his dearest friends. For Nietzsche, however, it is never too late for the adult to look back on his or her earlier youth with a mixture of suspicion and anger, so much so that the psyche in the present is also filled with self-doubt and mistrust. In Dante's Virgil, however, there is a statute of limitations on pity and self-recrimination. Dante, as we have seen, initially pities the souls in hell, only to be reprimanded by Virgil not to bestow such pity on fools who have wasted their time on earth and must pay for it eternally. For Freud, his dream was in itself enough punishment for the surviving remnants of his earlier grandiosity and greed, for his envy and imaginary aggressions against colleagues and rivals. It is only in the unconscious, where the longing for more time remains unchecked by reality, that Freud's erstwhile friends came back to haunt him with the prospect of being too late.

While Freud did seek to immerse the psyche in the residues of its old struggles and injuries, his purpose was not to secure for the infantile and androgynous self a heavenly transport but a rather sober emergence into the world of limits, of the passage of time, and of one's inevitable end. There are joys to be seized in such a Freudian world, but they are all the more precious for being fleeting rather than eternal. That is why the attempt to 'put away childish things' and to relinquish one's former self can degenerate into a chronic battle with time. Some prefer to protract their spiritual journeys and thus to continue an ambivalent relation to their past. Certainly to indulge in backward glances makes progress difficult, and any steps forward are then taken with more difficulty and trepidation. The one who is always on such a spiritual journey may also be daydreaming of a world full of magic and possibility rather than of barriers and limits. This longing for the primitive self may therefore even take the form of nostalgia for the magical kingdom of childhood. I will return to this aspect of the problem, and Freud's dream, once again, in Chapter 8, where I will discuss the search for a primitive self prior to any acquired or civilized character.

Freud discusses in some detail the problem of those who cannot seem to enjoy an adulthood that is free from the struggle with the earlier self and its longings for infinite possibility and enduring bliss.[18] Freud was particularly interested in a successful author named Rosegger who had begun life as a tailor. In one of his novels, Rosegger reported a recurrent dream in which he found himself, once again, a 'journeyman tailor' sitting beside his master, working long hours without pay. Even in the dream his adult self was present; he knew – in the dream itself – that in fact he was not a journeyman any longer but a 'townsman' and that he was 'always on vacation … always having holidays.'[19]

Thus in the dream his older self, personified as the master tailor, knew that he had better things to do with his time than to be an apprentice.[20]

Why, then, should Rosegger go through the self-mortification of being once again a 'journeyman' who is always daydreaming? Why perpetuate the chronic struggle between the adult who can take pride in his achievements and the 'journeyman' who still spends 'tedious hours,' without pay, in the master tailor's workshop?[21] There is in the dream a sense of wasting time: a recognition, I would suggest, that the older self is indeed wasting away and that it is time for the younger self to depart. Hence the journeyman in the dream reports that 'I felt sad at the loss of time in which I might well have found better and more useful things to do,' sad also, perhaps, at the loss of the earlier self that had been for so long a companion.[22] Perhaps the dream represents the last struggle of an earlier self who had thought he would last forever.

In the end, indeed, the youthful self is finally dispatched by 'the master' in the dream. Indeed, the master, like the adult Rosegger himself, is impatient with the apprentice and his continual daydreaming. Thus, in Rosegger's dream, the master fires the apprentice, and Rosegger the adult never has this dream again. *The struggle with the earlier self has ended, and Rosegger can take satisfaction in his adult achievements, both in his work and his family.*

There is some reason to doubt, however, whether Rosegger was finally ushered into the adult world without further conflict with his earlier self. Once the dreamer (journeyman) is dismissed from the cramped quarters of the workshop, an even younger journeyman replaces him: a Bohemian, 'a canting hypocrite,' who once fell into the water of a local brook. It is possible that an even earlier self is putting in an appearance, further to stimulate the adult's longings for more time and experience. Furthermore, in Rosegger's account of his journeyman dream, he wakes up to the sound of children in the next room having fun with their mother, and he scans his bookshelves with satisfaction at the sight of all the 'magnificent immortals,' Homer, Dante, Goethe and Shakespeare: famous authors like himself, a virtual treasure trove of time and experience. It may be that, in waking up, he arrives at a knowledge of his true place in life as a husband, a father, and as a writer who stands within a great tradition. It also may be, however, that he found resources in that tradition for further dreams of endless possibility.

It is therefore not clear whether Rosegger did in fact resolve his conflict with his earlier self. To be sure, he acknowledges that, after the dream of having been fired by the master, he never suffered again from this dream, which he had had repeatedly, and that he later experienced genuine freedom and release. He may not have relinquished, however, the wish to return to that androgynous, blissful, timeless experience of the primitive into which Goethe finally inducts Faust at his death. His longing for more time-without-end may have been expressed in the appearance of the Bohemian journeyman and in Rosegger's delight at re-joining Goethe and the other 'immortals.'

Why else would Rosegger's dream have contained notes of self-punishment: a judgement of the adult self on the grandiose daydreaming apprentice? As Freud suggests, Rosegger's dream punishes him for the infantile self's tendency to seduce the adult self into daydreams. That is why, I presume, that the master, as his more adult self, accuses him of 'wool-gathering.'[23] In describing a similar dream of his own, Freud concludes that '... the foundation of the dream was formed in the first instance by an exaggeratedly ambitious phantasy, but that humiliating thoughts that poured cold water on the phantasy found their way into the dream instead.'[24] The adult self does pour 'cold water' on the ambitions of one's youth, just as societies seek to keep the primitive at bay.

Certainly 'exaggeratedly ambitious fantasy' is an adult's way of describing the narcissistic striving and magical thinking of an earlier self. Thus Faust's journey begins with very ambitious fantasies indeed:

> Let's plunge into the torrents of time,
> into the whirl of eventful existence!
> There, as chance wills,
> let pain and pleasure,
> success and frustration, alternate;
> unceasing activity alone reveals our worth,

> I, ll.1754–59 ff.[25]

The soul engaged in a romantic journey is not open to the analytical self-scrutiny that is required by a more secular descent into the unconscious.

Remember that it is the devil, however, who sometimes stands for the fatherly 'reality-principle.' At least in the context of an 'exaggeratedly ambitious fantasy' those authorities who pour cold water on one's dreams may seem demonic. For instance, Faust imagines that he could be forever satisfied with his time on earth if he lived to see a particular accomplishment: an earthly Eden created by draining marshland and stemming the ocean's tide. Indeed, this vision fills him with enough ecstasy to qualify as his 'highest moment.' The analytical voice is then given to Mephistopheles, who pours instant cold water on 'this final, mediocre, empty moment –/the poor wretch wants to cling to it,' (I, ll.586; ll.589–590).[26] As Faust initially had proclaimed to Mephistopheles that, should his own enthusiasm for the journey end in a desire to prolong some exalted moment, he would want to die, Mephistopheles announces that

> 'He who resisted me with such great vigor
> – time triumphs – lies here on the sand an old, old man.
> The clock stands still,'

> I, ll.586; ll.591–593[27]

The primitive father returns to announce the victory of time: the father disguised as the devil who reminds one of the passage of time and of the inevitability of death.

The devil is an ambivalent image of the father as the one who sets limits on all others' desires, who opposes the grandiose, younger self, and who enjoys a monopoly on illegitimate satisfaction. Thus Freud goes on to note that there is a conflict in many dreams 'between a *parvenu's* pride and his self-criticism ...' After all, that conflict is precisely what reality itself produces as one emerges, finally, into the present. Only with renunciation of primitive desire is the soul free from the burden of the past and from the moribund parts of the psyche. Until that moment, the adult self continues to be locked into a struggle with the younger. Indeed Freud refers to some of his own dreams as 'the punishment dreams of a *parvenu*, like the dreams of the journeyman tailor who had grown into a famous author.'[28] These dreams, Freud notes, are 'disagreeable in the same way as examination dreams and they are never very distinct.'[29]

What, then, is behind the desire to perpetuate the quarrel with one's past self? It is the longing to recover primitive vitality, original virtue, and the lost self that seemed immune, at least in fantasy, to the passage of time. It is this search for excluded possibility that becomes more hopeless and pressing as one enters middle-age and experiences the beginning of the end of one's time. Speaking of another punishment dream, in which he was thrown back to his own days as an assistant in a chemical laboratory, Freud remarks:

> The unconscious instigator of the dream was thus revealed as one of the constantly gnawing wishes of a man who is growing older. The conflict raging in other levels of the mind between vanity and self-criticism had, it is true, determined the content of the dream; but it was only the more deeply rooted wish for youth that had made it possible for that wish to appear as a dream.[30]

Freud is writing as a man who is waking up from the dream of living a life of endless possibility.

For Freud, the conflict with the younger self is simply a waste of time. That places Freud in opposition to Nietzsche, who appears never to have given up his wish for a life in time that never ends. Thus Nietzsche disavows any 'ill will' toward the temporal, but his disavowal is not convincing. As Genevieve Lloyd puts it, his belief in 'eternal return'

> offers a redemption not from time but from 'the will's ill will towards time' with its ceaseless 'it was.' 'Ill will' towards time degrades all that passes away, treating the transient as a form of non-being, in contrast to the true Being of the permanent ...

> The desire for eternal return is, rather, the longing that is implicit in joy, with its delight in the present. 'Joy, however, does not want heirs, or children, joy wants itself, wants eternity, wants recurrence, wants everything eternally the same.'[31]

No 'ill will' toward time and yet a wish for everything always to be the same? 'The affirmation of eternal return is an affirmation of the present, a refusal to let it drain away in the hope of a better future or a release from present suffering.'[32] What is meant, it would appear, is a Faustian plunge into time without the experience of a single moment that would last forever, yet every suffering is repeated and no joy ever lost. It would be difficult to find a more exact illustration of the primitive terrain of the unconscious and of the fantasies of youth. Thus Lloyd summarizes the point: 'For if the future takes on something of the fixity of the past in this Nietzschean convergence of being and becoming, it is no less true that the past loses some of its separation from the life and vivacity of the present.'[33]

Lost time, for Nietzsche, is therefore never lost; it is always returning:

> Even in his mature thought Nietzsche seems to see no real inconsistency between eternal recurrence and uniqueness. Indeed, he seems to see the juxtaposition of unrepeatability and recurrence as the core of the doctrine. It is in their very uniqueness that he wants to see individual events as eternally recurring – not in some remote future time where the 'variegated assortment that we are' is reformed, but in the here and now.[34]

How can the past be both past and present, unique and yet repeatable? Lloyd later finds it 'mind-numbing' to try to make sense of Nietzsche's idea of a past.[35] 'Mind-numbing' though it may be, this attempt to have it both ways exemplifies the capacity of the primitive to imagine victories over the limits of space and time.

To enter fully into the unconscious requires one to experience those parts of the self that are so steeped in fantasy and longing that they seem to have an autonomous will of their own and thus are able to persist without the active permission of the adult self. Nietzsche, Lloyd notes, does not have a role for 'a transcendent will as to what kinds of thing are worthy of its choice;' there is no call for the will to choose 'what *kinds* of event it will endorse.'[36] Between the grandiosity of the self that sees everything under the aspect of eternity, and the dreamy or romping junior self that never takes no for an answer, there is little space left for the will.

Freud understood that the past does indeed have a way of pressing into the present and of shaping the future; old battles and old loves come back, as it were, eternally, and he noted the tendency to repeat unpleasant experiences as well as to return to scenes loaded with images of an imaginary crime or a primal scene. However, it is these tendencies, as we have seen, that keep one from ever arriving in time, in the present, as a master of oneself. So long as the past eternally returns, one remains a 'journeyman,' the perennial *'parvenu'* who is always late.[37]

## Notes

1 Janine Chasseguet-Smirgel (1984), *Creativity and Perversion*, Foreword by Otto Kernberg, New York, London: W. W. Norton and Company.
2 *The Inferno of Dante*, a new verse translation by Robert Pinsky with Notes by Nicole Pinsky, Foreword by John Freccero (1994), New York: The Noonday Press, Farrar, Straus and Giroux, p. 105.
3 Ibid., p. 105.
4 Ibid., pp. 105 (first quotation), 103 (second quotation).
5 Stuart Atkins (1984), *Goethe, The Collected Works*, Princeton, NJ: Princeton University Press, p. 30.
6 Ibid., pp. 53 ff., 60 ff.
7 Ibid., p. 65.
8 Ibid., p. 62.
9 Ibid., p. 295.
10 Ibid., p. 296.
11 Ibid., p. 296.
12 The connection between narcissism and masochism has been developed by Arnold M. Cooper (1998); see 'The Narcissitic-Masochistic Character,' in Robert A. Glick and Donald I. Meyers (eds.), *Masochism: Current Psychoanalytic Perspectives*, Hillsdale, NJ, London: The Analytic Press, pp. 117–38.
13 Friedrich Nietzsche, *Beyond Good and Evil. Prelude to a Philosophy of the Future*, Translated, and with Commentary by Walter Kaufmann (1966), New York: Vintage Books, p. 43.
14 Ibid.
15 Sigmund Freud (1965), *The Interpretation of Dreams*, New York: Avon Books (A Division of The Hearst Corporation), pp. 456–7.
16 Ibid., p. 458.
17 Ibid., p. 519.
18 Ibid., pp. 510–15.
19 Ibid., p. 511.
20 Ibid.
21 Ibid.
22 Ibid.
23 Ibid., p. 512.
24 Ibid., p. 513.
25 Atkins, op. cit., p. 45.
26 Ibid., p. 292.
27 Ibid.
28 Freud, op. cit., p. 513.
29 Ibid.
30 Ibid., p. 514.
31 Genevieve Lloyd (1993), *Being in Time*, New York and London: Routledge, pp. 117–18; quotation from Friedrich Nietzsche, *Thus Spake Zarathrustra*, Book IV, Section 19, sub-section 9, translated by R. J. Hollingdale (1991), London: Penguin, p. 331.

32  Lloyd, op. cit., p. 118.
33  Ibid.
34  Ibid., p. 108.
35  Ibid., p. 110.
36  Ibid., pp. 110–11.
37  Freud, op. cit., p. 117.

Chapter 7

# The Descent into the Unconscious as Unauthorized Self-possession: The Recovery of the Lost and Dying Self

In the preceding chapter, I suggested that one of the functions of religious language is to embrace, express and overcome the conflict between the more mature and the more primitive aspects of the psyche. The danger is simply that the religious language, by embodying excluded possibilities, will keep people confused about the limits of possibility. That potential is both its strength and its ultimate weakness. As Paul Dutton notes of dreamers during the Carolingian period, their world was one of 'intimate dimensions, where both sinners and saints could be seen with a sweep of the eyes … For sinners, the proximity of the blessed added immeasurably to their sufferings.'[1] Possibilities for sanctity and for the satisfaction of desire were tangibly present even when they were inaccessible, given the condition of one's soul. The religious could never rest in the confident possession of their souls but must engage in preventive lamentation, lest they, too, be consigned to those who would be forever tormented by impossible desire.

Without the capacity to recover and embody the primitive, religious language remains a dialectic of conventional speech, in which religious intellectuals discuss ideas and events, dilemmas and moral problems, within the framework of what is conventionally considered possible. Reinhold Niebuhr, for example, derided those who were anything but realistic about the facts of politics and power in the twentieth century, and he regarded idealism as naïve and potentially dangerous. Theologians seek scientific support for their viewpoints, and ethicists rely on sociologists for their generalizations about social structures and processes. Even religious intellectuals in the eighth and ninth centuries who made use of dream-like visions were very quick to distance themselves from dreams and visionary language. Alcuin, a poet in the service of the court of Charlemagne, used the *Vision of Drythelm* as a source for his own poetic understanding of the descent into hell. I will take up that vision in this chapter. Here it is important to remember that Alcuin also argued that 'those who believe in dreams give themselves up to vanity and folly.'[2] Although he himself apparently had had ecstatic visions that foretold the future, he thought such visions too dangerous for the ordinary. It was a convention of the Carolingian period, as we have seen, to believe that dreaming was best reserved for those who were qualified by sanctity or kingship.

This tendency to exclude the ordinary from the inspiration and authority that comes from dreams and dreaming has its own dangers. Those who are deprived of the authority to dream on their own and to interpret their own dreams will nevertheless be restive under the constraints of what passes for realistic expectation. They will find their own visionaries, who dream of a day of judgement and retribution. Those who lack their own visions will find themselves attuned to those who promise an apocalyptic age of otherwise unimaginable satisfaction for those who have been excluded from the prevailing distribution of honor and satisfactions. The primitive, the peasants with pitchforks who stormed medieval cities to kill the burghers and the clergy, always return.

However, it is too late to be naïve about the magical thinking, the grandiosity, and delusions, the underlying cruelty and impossible longings that do in fact come coded in dreams. It is too late to act or think as if the twentieth century and the psychoanalytic movement had not happened. Thus if religious language is to be allowed to incorporate the language of the dream, it will be necessary for those who employ it to become literate about the unconscious. That is, it will be necessary for those who speak the language of the dream to become familiar once again with the underground terrain of the unconscious.

I say 'once again' because there was indeed a time when the subterranean aspects of the psyche were well known and even part of common parlance. However, they were disguised as part of an underground universe that could be explored only by a trained guide, a shaman, who undertook a descent, a *katabasis*, to the infernal regions; Pythagoras appears to have been one of the earliest types who claimed that ' "he had been down to Hades, and even read out his experiences …" '[3] As Guy Stroumsa has argued, however, the notion of a descent into hell as being the soul's own mystical journey long escaped the control of shamanism and became the common property of a wide range of religious traditions.[4] Focussed frequently on caves, the pious and the searcher would lower sacred gifts into these or descend into them themselves as pilgrims in search of oracles or an inner change. This hunger for revelation or transformation was apparently as widespread among Jews as among Greeks, and the relationships among the several traditions in this regard remain complex and not wholly understood, but it would be premature to assume that Jewish and Greek versions of the descent into the underworld were wholly independent of one another.[5] What is clear is that a spiritual and often physical pilgrimage to the underworld was part and parcel of the soul's journey inward to its own subconscious foundations.

What, then, could have severed this link between a spiritual journey downward and the soul's own discovery of its own most primitive origins? The answer, of course, depends on how particular societies managed their own relations to the primitive. That is, the fate of the descent into hell depends on the particular ways that societies construe the primitive and thus exclude certain possibilities. In the case of the classical descent into hell, the loss of this form of spiritual inquiry into the soul's underlying foundations would have been the result of a wide range of policies and processes in the years of Constantine and in centuries following. No doubt the Eastern Church, for instance, was more hospitable to the journey of the soul inward and downward than the West even before Constantine; Stroumsa speaks of Ephrem, for instance, as a fourth-century Syriac source for the spiritual descent into hell.[6] Under Constantine, moreover, there was an attempt to root out pagan devotions located in caves.[7] Augustine himself, in his attacks on pagans and especially on Manichaeans, would have been a major influence in suppressing the spiritual descent into hell. Indeed, Stroumsa notes that Augustine linked the journey inward with the 'mystical ascent' to heaven rather than a descent into hell.[8] Stroumsa summarizes this fundamental and crucial shift in the direction of the soul's spiritual journey:

> The *unio mystica,* or rather the *way* leading to it, would usually be perceived, from now on, essentially through two different but combined metaphors, one the metaphor of going up, or ascent, and the other that of going inside, or interiorization ... In the new thought patterns emerging from this transformation, the earlier metaphor of descent retained no clear function, and its *Fortleben* was more literary than religious, directly linked as it was to Virgil's role model in European medieval literature. This influence, up to Dante, cannot be overemphasized.[9]

That is why, later in this chapter, we will return to Dante in order to develop further a notion of a spiritual descent into hell, albeit one under the guidance of Virgil rather than of Freud.

Certainly the notion of a spiritual descent into hell became literary, and if Stroumsa is right, even the early medieval visions of a spiritual descent into hell, like the *Vision of Drythelm*, will be understood only if we see them as continuations of the original descents of earlier Jewish, Greek and even Scythian antiquity.[10] That is, if the Constantinian and later Church construed paganism as primitive and thus excluded the spiritual descent into hell as a possibility for the soul, it would not be surprising if such a descent was therefore relegated precisely to the underworld of the dream.

It is one thing for religious language to keep alive the possibility of recovering parts of the self that, because they have been split off, have become moribund or mortified. It is quite another, however, to engage in the act of will that is necessary to undertake the descent into the unconscious to recover these parts of the self or, conversely, if necessary to let them go or altogether to renounce them. In certain early medieval visions of the spiritual underworld, the visions of Drythelm and of Wetti, we will find religious language engaging in all three functions of descent, recovery and finally of renunciation. They are functions that are performed, for the most part, by ordinary men and women seeking to repossess their own souls. However, in at least one of these visions, we find traces of an attempt by the Church to appropriate the lay person's spiritual journey for its own use by encouraging submission to ecclesiastical guidance and discipline.

In Drythelm's vision, a man is reported to have died one evening after an illness, and then, the next morning, somewhat to the surprise or even horror of his grieving family, awakened from the dead. After bequeathing all his property to his wife and family, and to the poor, he took the tonsure and finished his days in a monastery, where he was known to have told a tale of descending into hell. There he witnessed the torments of souls:

> ... I observed a gang of evil spirits dragging the howling and lamenting souls of people into the middle of the darkness, while the devils themselves laughed and rejoiced. Among the people, from what I could see, there was one shorn like a clergyman, a layman and a woman. The evil spirits who dragged them went down into the midst of the burning pit; and as they went down deeper, I could no longer distinguish between the lamentation of the people and the laughing of the devils, yet I still had a confused sound in my ears.[11]

Indeed, the visitor, Drythelm himself, is in danger of being tormented by these same devils, but he is rescued in time by his angelic guide, who later explains that what he there has seen '... is the mouth of hell, and whoever falls into it shall never be delivered for all eternity.'[12]

Certainly we have here a suggestion that the dreamer and visionary is at the place where one might recover aspects of the soul that have long been lost. The dream or vision itself describes hell in the very realistic sense of being a place of continuing and endless torment in which it is always too late for any hope of redemption: indeed too late for release or satisfaction of any kind. However, the intensity of lamentation suggests that hopeless desire also never diminishes. There one is tormented by intense and continuing desire for which there is no possible satisfaction, because desire maintains its possession of the soul. In this sense, then, hell is a place in which time never passes.

The primitive returns in this vision as the excluded possibility that is nonetheless embodied in the suffering of the tormented soul. On the one hand the soul continues to long for the impossible. On the other hand it is tormented by devils that are the very reminder that one can never have what one desires. The two, the longing and the torment, become indistinguishable, just as Drythelm found it impossibly hard to 'distinguish between the lamentation of the people and the laughing of the devils.'

The *Vision of Drythelm* also suggests the possibility, however, of recovering these aspects of the soul that, however tormented or moribund they may be, are not wholly beyond hope of rescue and relief. Later in the vision, for instance, Drythelm goes on to find an enormous wall that at first seems insurmountable, but as in a dream the impossible is actualized, so Drythelm suddenly finds himself atop the wall with his angelic guide. From there they witness the happiness of souls waiting for admission into the kingdom of heaven: a possibility from which those on the tormented side of the wall are excluded. Thus, in the dream itself, the dreamer transcends this division between the possible and the impossible. Indeed he acts out the transcendence of such division in the most literal and visual of terms, by standing on top of a wall.

In the *Vision of Drythelm*, then, we may have elements of an earlier story of a spiritual journey into the world of life after death: a story that has been overlaid by later years of ecclesiastical editing and revision. The soul of Drythelm, during its sojourn from the body, is originally met by someone with 'a shining countenance and a bright garment': not a figure that was clearly defined as part of the Church's pantheon, such as a well-known angel or saint.[13] Furthermore, Drythelm's soul thinks at first that he is going toward 'the place where the sun rises on the solstice': perhaps a reminiscence of pre-Christian religious practices.[14] In the darkness and the fire, where the cries of the souls were mingled with the laughing of the 'evil spirits,' Drythelm's soul sees 'a clergyman, a layman and a woman': relatively ordinary people rather than the kings and nobles who in later visions suffered horribly for their crimes against the Church.[15] Again, the scenes seem to be those of daily life: not palaces and fine dwellings so much as a valley consumed with fire and cold, a shining star, a wall, and a field with a secret garden: visionary commonplaces.

Toward the end of the tale, however, there are signs of what may well be later ecclesiastical redaction. Much as the editors of the gospel narratives portrayed Jesus as having asked the disciples whether or not they understood the parable that he had told them, the text here shows signs of an editor who adds:

When we returned to those joyful mansions of the souls in white, he [the guide] said to me, 'Do you know what all these things are that you have seen?'

I answered that I did not; and then he replied, 'That valley you saw so dreadful because of the consuming flames and cutting cold is the place to try and punish the souls of those who delay to confess and amend their sins, but eventually have recourse to repentance at the point of death, and so depart from this life ...'[16]

The guide continues with certain reassurances that confessions just before death qualify souls for entrance into the kingdom of heaven on the Day of Judgment, but other souls have less long to wait if they are 'aided before the Day of Judgment by the prayers, alms and fasting of the living, and more especially by Masses.'[17] The Church's interest in prescribing duties to the faithful and in insisting on practices that strengthen the Church itself is more than evident. It is an interest that Martha Himmelfarb has detected in more ancient 'tours of hell.'[18] Even the presence of a higher authority that dispenses a sort of justice to the departed souls is present in the guide's explanation that he had left the soul of Drythelm temporarily 'to know how you were to be disposed of.'[19]

There is some reason to think that other traditions also have experienced this tension between accounts by ordinary people of their own spiritual journeys and descents into hell, on the one hand, and on the other hand the accounts favored by religious officials. Robert Ford Campany has found a number of Chinese tales 'written by and about laypersons of the lower and middle strata of the official class or ordinary monks and nuns': tales of their spiritual journeys to the other world.[20] These tales are marked by their simplicity, by the ordinariness and familiarity of the scenes and persons they describe, and by the accessibility of the other world to the ordinary soul. They resemble the *Vision of Drythelm* without the admonitions and prescriptions to engage in certain practices to ensure the welfare of the soul before and during the Day of Judgment. Especially in valuing this life over the next they share a common spirit.

The more authoritative Chinese texts, Buddhist and Taoist alike, however, find the soul's fate determined either by spiritual virtuosi or by otherworldly bureaucrats and lesser deities. One can only alter one's fate in the other world by claiming that one needs more time to study the bureaucracy's procedures or to become adept at certain spiritual practices.[21] Similarly, the Buddhist tales emphasize the need of the soul to realize 'the reality and gravity of Buddhist teachings concerning karmic retribution,' as opposed to the non-Buddhist tales that avoid such admonishments and exhibit simply 'a healthy conviction that the soul survives death and may be judged according to its merits and faults.'[22]

There is, then, a certain populism in some of the tales of a journey to the underworld. In the *Vision of Wetti*, another dream of the Carolingian period, a monk rounds up some of those usually held suspect in the popular imagination: counts who offer justice 'for sale, just like their souls,' bishops and abbots who were indifferent to the suffering of other souls, both dead and alive; priests '... who do not concern themselves with gaining their souls;' and a bishop who callously stated that 'the deliriums of dreams are not to be listened to ....'[23] These reformist elements are obvious, and they suggest that the dream of a descent into the underworld remained a source of inspiration and authority for those within the Church whose presence may well have been overshadowed by the more influential abbots and bishops and their allies among the rival counts of the Carolingian period. Indeed, Paul Dutton points out that

> The *Vision of Wetti* became the most famous of all Carolingian dreams, and there was a flowering of dream literature in the ninth century. That aforementioned poet of Charlemagne's court, Alcuin, whose 'attitude toward dreams and visions always remained stubbornly cautious' and who wished 'to limit the this-worldly implications of discourse with the otherworld' nonetheless 'admitted that what mattered in the end was the truth of the dream' ... Thus even the skeptics lived in a world where it was difficult to deny the existence of powerful and probative dreams.[24]

If religious language is to recover the power of the dream, then, and reveal what dreamers know about their own descents into a hell of impossible and hopeless desire, it will have to avoid the auspices of the Church, with its interest in disciplining individuals and in limiting their aspirations for self-healing. The discourse of religious language will also have to avoid the constraints imposed by professionals, whose visions so often convey the implicit message that ordinary dreamers need the guidance of the extraordinary virtuoso and of the spiritual adept. Neither the disciplines of a seer or the penances imposed by an ecclesiastical bureaucracy, however, have been able to eclipse the record in tales such as the visions of Drythelm and Wetti: the record of ordinary lay persons and monks whose conversations with the other world did not at first conform to authorized versions.

I do not mean to idealize the lay person's own spiritual courage and ability to undertake, unaided by guidance of any sort, a descent into the underworld of the psyche. I do mean, however, to suggest that the stakes are simply the possession of the soul. That is, will individuals be able literally to call their souls their own or will they be allowed a vicarious sort of possession of their souls under the supervision of spiritual adepts, gurus, or of Church officials with a vested interest in the obedience of the laity to the Church's penitential discipline? The interest of the *Vision of Drythelm* is clear: 'that the living may be saved from the death of the soul.'[25] That interest, I would argue, is precisely where his vision overlaps with that of Freud and later psychoanalysis. Souls can die long before their owners perish, and it is to avoid that spiritual death that one undertakes a descent into the underworld of the psyche and meets one's own passions without demonizing them.

The notion that one has a true self that can become lost through a series of wrong decisions and the perversion of the will – a self that can be recovered through a spiritual pilgrimage – is as old as the monastic disciplines and as perennial as Dante's own sentiment: 'Midway on our life's journey, I found myself/In dark woods, the right road lost,' (Canto I.1–2).[26] To recover that self requires a spiritual journey to one's past, in which one may encounter the primitive in the form of the bizarre and ghoulish, or the merely vacuous and pretentious aspects of a long-forgotten self.

In that mid-life valley to which Dante refers there is a recognition that what one has thought would give one a full life is in fact empty, and one is in danger oneself of becoming the mere shell of one's former self. That same sentiment was also fundamental, as we have seen, to Freud, who stands in the tradition of Goethe and Dante in arguing that there is a true self hidden under the armor of character. That inner self may only emerge under the right conditions, but it can be forever lost under the weight of injury, loss and propriety. In fleeing from the past, as it is embodied in one's character, one may look back on one's earlier ambitions only to find them full of destructive fantasies about eliminating others: full also of tendencies toward self-mortification and self-sacrifice. The search for the lost self may therefore be perilous, even destructive, but it is imperative. Otherwise one is left to the unconvincing and unsatisfying devices of self-invention, or to self-destruction in despair ever of ridding the self from the burden of acquired character. If the past holds the secret of the present, it is still, as Faust puts it, 'a book with seven seals,' (I, 1.576).[27] It must therefore be opened with care if one is not to be destroyed in the attempt to find the true self that, in the course of time, has been forfeited.

When the self has become embodied in social character, it is kept there behind various 'seals:' by the pain of old injuries; by longings that have not yet been acknowledged, let alone fulfilled; by imaginary crimes that one has committed only in fantasy; by desires to recover the timeless satisfactions of earliest infancy, to name only a few. That is why the search for one's soul is also perilous, if only because it can be made to serve self-destructive tendencies rather than fulfill the original intent of the quest. Remember that, in Goethe's *Faust*, Mephistopheles boasts in his thirst for authentic and vital selfhood, that Faust would destroy himself in the end – 'even if he had no contract with the devil,/ he'd end up ruined anyhow!' (I, ll.1866–67).[28]

It is not only social character, however, that creates a prison from the materials of the past. Something more than the passage of time may have closed the door of possibility. To be sure, it may also be too late in any realistic sense to satisfy certain longings: the one we loved has died, or we are no longer able to act on old affections, even though they persist. However, it may also be too late fully to recover one's soul if crucial parts of the self have died along the way. Perhaps one has been reduced to nothing by a rebuke, as we have seen in the case of Freud, or by a beatific vision, as Dante reported of his ecstatic love for Beatrice. Perhaps one has split off a part of the self that is otherwise too intense or painful for one to bear, and it is now someone else who is seen as dangerous or compassionate, vital or demonic, rather than oneself. It is these psychic deaths that also make it 'too late' for one to fulfill old longings and that create a certain despair over the passage of time: the chronic feeling of being late.

The dangers of the psyche's effort to avoid pain are most visible in extreme cases. For instance, in speaking of abused children, Ferenczi notes '... a last, desperate attempt to adapt, perhaps analogous to the feigning of death in animals ...:'

> The person splits into a psychic being of pure knowledge that observes the events from the outside, and a totally insensitive body. Insofar as this psychic being is still accessible to emotions, it turns its interests toward the only feelings left over from the process, that is, the feelings of the attacker. It is as though the psyche, whose sole function is to reduce emotional tensions and to avoid pain, at the moment of the death of its own person automatically diverts its pain-relieving functions toward the pains, tensions, and passions of the attacker, the only person with feelings, that is, and identifies with these.[29]

To recover one's soul, then it is necessary to experience those parts of the self that have been separated from one's own psyche and attributed to others, where they remain hidden and can be enjoyed only vicariously. The inner self, first numbed and then absent from direct experience, is projected into others, where it lives a surrogate existence in disguise. Serving others then becomes a long and indirect route to self-recovery. As Ferenczi puts it:

> The disappearance of one's own person, while others are still present in the scene, would thus be at the deepest root of masochism (otherwise so puzzling), of self-sacrifice for other people, animals, or things, or of the identification with outside tensions and pains that is nonsensical from a psychological or egoistic point of view.[30]

This masochistic self-sacrifice is particularly characteristic of those who as children have been abused by those whom they had loved and trusted. Indeed, as early as 1932, Ferenczi had understood that the self dies at least a partial death in an effort to save itself from its own overwhelming anguish, grief and terror. Thus Ferenczi speaks of a masochistic tendency which is as fundamentally self-destructive as a Faustian plunge into long-delayed experience in an effort to revive a moribund psyche.

Faust's attempts to 'plunge into the torrents of time,' to leave behind the boring intellectual pursuits of the middle-aged and to find the vitality of perennial youth, do indeed appear on the surface to be wholly narcissistic. However, there is a hint of a more desperate quest to recover a psyche that has been on the verge of death. Faust had been at the point of holding in his hands a suicidal cup of poison when he was distracted by the sounds of others' Easter joy. Numb to his own emotions, he begins to recover himself only through the vicarious experience of contemplating the humanity of others. To be sure, Faust vows to undertake the full range of human experience, but it requires a surrogate, Mephistopheles, to let him enter into its mysteries. At the very least Faust's narcissism has been wounded, and he wishes no longer to feel that he is small, or that his knowledge is insignificant, or that his experience is useless to any one else, or that he is dwarfed by a universe of unimaginable size and complexity.

However, underlying this attempt to invent or remake the self are strong masochistic tendencies to deny or displace the inner self with all its own uncertainty and anguish.[31] The extreme narcissist subordinates, denies and displaces the self, and so seeks to immunize it from grief and sorrow. The repression necessary to sustain this immunity may numb the self to death. As Ferenczi puts it:

> no masochistic action or emotional impulse of the sort is possible without the temporary dying of one's own person. So I do not feel the pain inflicted upon me at all, because I do not exist. On the other hand I do feel the pleasure-gratification of the attacker, which I am still able to perceive. The fundamental thesis of all psychology, that the sole function of the psyche is to reduce pain, is therefore preserved. The pain-alleviating function must, however, be able to apply itself not only to one's own ego but also to every kind of pain perceived or imagined by the psyche.[32]

Thus ordinary attempts to feel, through the excitement, pleasure or suffering of others, are, as Ferenczi suggests, attempts to resuscitate what is left of a self that has been cut off from its own wells of emotion. This is the bargain with the devil, so to speak: a way of buying time for a surrogate existence rather than a recovery of one's own suffering pysche.

Ferenczi's notion of a 'temporary dying of one's own person,' like his suggestion that there is a '... disappearance of one's own person, while others are still present in the scene' (quoted above), elaborates his concept of the 'death agony' of the neurotic psyche that represses or splits off part of the self that is too painful or repugnant to be assimilated into the conscious psyche. However, the possibility of losing one's soul in the presence of others who represent an overpowering attraction or threat is not limited to the neurotic, just as it is not confined to cases of sexual or mental abuse. Nonetheless in these more extreme cases the tendency to self-mortification is most readily visible. Consider Ferenczi's description of a patient who as a little girl had been sexually attacked by her father. In her nightmares this patient had resisted these attacks as long as she could:

> But suddenly her will power gives way, and at the same moment complete numbness sets in with regard to her own self, but without her losing any awareness of the whole scene; on the contrary, she now sees the whole event as though from the outside; she sees a dead child being abused in the manner just described. With the state of being 'dead' even pity, quite remarkably (and of course fear, rescue attempts, etc.) ceases completely; instead, interest, even feeling, and complete understanding are now diverted to the aggressor. She finds it self-evident that the accumulation of tensions in the attacker had to be discharged in the way described.[33]

The woman herself acknowledged to Ferenczi that she regarded a part of herself as 'dead.' She was already 'late.' Indeed, Ferenczi's patient imitated her own death while she was recounting her nightmares and her recollections of sexual abuse by her father. She became deathly herself, even as she described the dead child of her dreams.

That is why Ferenczi emphasized the collapse and recovery of the will. Without the will, so to speak, the person is as good as dead; only in a revival of the will does the individual begin again to come alive. There seems to have been a new rush of vitality in patients when they were able to prevail over Ferenczi with regard to the conduct of their analysis. Certainly individuals who as children were abused by adults were at the time of their suffering somewhat paralyzed, whether by being entranced, frightened, or overwhelmed with pain. As a result, the memory itself will include elements of distortion and inertia that make it difficult for the individual later to perceive his or her will in operation at the time of the original trauma. Indeed, it is as if part of the person may have been frozen or died at the moment of the traumatic encounter and is permanently beyond recall through psychoanalysis or hypnosis. Like the soul that descends into hell in some of the medieval visions, the inner self may indeed disappear and yearn for divine rescue.

This sort of self-mortification can be developed into a taste for permanent anesthesia of the soul. Unless by an act of the will the living allow the departed actually to depart, individuals will continue to exist in a state of perpetual, however partial, self-mortification. As in Dante's descent into hell, the individual may feel unable or forbidden to muster the emotional power to pity. Only by an act of the will, then, could one suffer grief and feel pity and compassion without the anodyne of narcissistic or magical thinking. By the same argument, it is only by an act of will that the individual who is able to suffer repressed memories and feelings will not only recover these aspects of the self but also let them atrophy and die a natural death rather than a death by self-alienation. Without such an act of the will and a willingness therefore to suffer loss without hope of restoration, one may protract self-mortification indefinitely.

## Notes

1 Paul Dutton (1994), *The Politics of Dreaming in the Carolingian Empire*, Lincoln and London: The University of Nebraska Press, pp. 60–61.

2 Alcuin, *Commentaria super Ecclesiasten* (in Eccles. 5.6), quoted in Paul Dutton (1994), *The Politics of Dreaming in the Carolingian Empire*, p. 44.

3 Guy C. Stroumsa (1995), 'Mystical Descents,' in John C. Collins and Michael Fishbane (eds.), *Death, Ecstasy, and Other Worldly Journeys*, Albany, NY: State University of New York Press, p. 140.

4 Ibid., pp. 141 ff.

5 Ibid., p. 146.

6 Ibid., p. 144.

7 Ibid., p. 143.

8 Ibid., p. 147.

9 Ibid.

10 Ibid., p. 140.

11 'Drythelm's Vision,' in Eileen Gardiner (ed.) (1989), *Visions of Heaven and Hell Before Dante*, New York: Italic Press, p. 59.

12 Ibid., p. 61.

13 Ibid., p. 58.

14 Ibid.

15 Ibid., p. 59.

16 Ibid., p. 61.

17 Ibid., p. 61.

18 Martha Himmelfarb (1983), *Tours of Hell. An Apocalyptic Form in Jewish and Christian Literature*, Philadelphia: University of Pennsylvania Press, p. 122.

19 'Drythelm's Vision,' op. cit., p. 62.

20 Robert Ford Campany (1995), 'To Hell and Back: Death, Near-Death, and Other Worldly Journeys in Early Medieval China,' in John C. Collins and Michael Fishbane (eds.), *Death, Ecstasy, and Other Worldly Journeys*, Albany, NY: State University of New York Press, p. 345.

21 Ibid., p. 349.

22 Ibid., p. 353.

23 'Wetti's Vision,' in Gardiner (ed.), op. cit., pp. 68, 70, 72.

24 Dutton, op. cit., pp. 44, 43, 45.

25 'Drythelm's Vision,' in Gardiner (ed.), op. cit., p. 57.

26 *The Inferno of Dante*, a new verse translation by Robert Pinsky with Notes by Nicole Pinsky, Foreword by John Freccero (1994), New York: The Noonday Press, Farrar, Straus and Giroux, p. 1.

27 Ibid., p. 18.

28 Ibid., p. 48.

29 Ferenczi (1995), *The Clinical Diary of Sandor Ferenczi*, Cambridge, Mass. and London, England: Harvard University Press, p. 104.

30 Ibid.

31 Arnold Cooper, "The Narcissistic–Masochistic Character", in Robert A. Glick and Donald I. Meyers (1988), *Masochism: Current Psychoanalytic Perspectives.*
32 Ferenczi, op. cit., p. 104.
33 Ibid., p. 103.

# Chapter 8

# Preventing the Death of the Soul: Freud's Descent into the Realm of the Unconscious

To offer a pathway to the primitive aspects of the psyche remains the task of religious guidance, but the guides can no longer be early Christian ascetics, early medieval visionaries, Dante or more modern romantics. Despite their familiarity with the netherworld of the soul, they provide recourse to delusions and magical thinking. The journey to the primitive psyche will have to be undertaken with one thought in mind, that the purpose of the journey is to prevent the death of the soul. Therefore the journey itself must not fall under the spell of infantile longings and delusions or to attempts to immunize the psyche against pain. Dante was still willing to let Virgil censure his pity even though it was Virgil who also kept deciphering what was left unspoken by Dante himself.

The point of Freud's descent into the hell of the unconscious, however, is to recover pity for a self that had long been mortified and may have been moribund. In that descent he encounters the infantile self of murderous rivalry and of unrealistic desires that seeks to keep old loves alive forever. Moreover, even that infantile core is the nucleus of the inner self, before the psyche was overlaid by acceptable social character and transformed through sublimation. In the long run that early, primitive self will be abandoned, but the path to the recovery of the psyche first requires that one enter into the old desires and torments and into the field of grief and remorse.

The longing to recover a more primitive self underlies the desire to undertake many a spiritual journey. One goes in search of a self that was originally felt to be innocent, potent and spontaneous: a soul that was given rather than acquired; substantial rather than a play of appearances; full of promise and therefore averse to limitation. The pathway to such a self, however, takes one into a primitive world from which the father has been eliminated: the father being the set of conventional limitations as well as the sign of mature potency. One is left to one's own passions endlessly, as it were, in the absence of the father's pitiless control. That is, one repeats the primordial crime of eliminating the father and being left only with others equally in torment as oneself. One can experience unalloyed passion far from the surveillance of the divine but only under the domain of a bad, that is a satanic, conscience. Instead of remaining in the father's presence, therefore, one encounters a demonic patriarch in whose eternal control one lives without hope of respite or return: Satan himself.

That is, in seeking to recover a primitive self one may even imagine that it is possible to go back before the onset of the awareness of irreversible separation and personal limitation to a self that is fully engaged with others in relationships and loves that will never pass away. At this antecedent level of the psyche, one remains passionate in a timeless universe, where the only people who worry about the passage of time are occasional visitors like Virgil and Dante: visitors from another world where time does indeed run out. They are signs, I would argue, that the descent into hell may disguise an attempt to recover the experience of the youthful self, before civilization had taken too deep a bite out of one's desires and imagination, and before reality had presented too forceful a reminder of limitations and the eventual moment when time runs out on everyone.

It is the desire for a prelapsarian self that will never be late, never run out of time, and thus never die, that feeds the fires of hopeless passions. Such a desire can take many forms, but in this chapter we will return to Freud himself, whose own descent into the unconscious uncovered a number of figures who were ostensibly dead but who kept coming back. With them they brought a new reminder of old loves and hatreds that, Freud admitted, had not passed away.

Remember the dream of Freud's that we discussed in Chapter 6, in which he gives a mortifying glance to an old colleague. For the convenience of the reader I quote the passage about the dream again here, since the details are important for our discussion:

I had gone to Brucke's laboratory at night, and, in response to a gentle knock on the door, I opened it to (*the late*) Professor Fleischl, who came in with a number of strangers and, after exchanging a few words, sat down at his table. This was followed by a second dream. My friend Fl. [Fliess] had come to Vienna unobtrusively in July. I met him in the street in conversation with my (*deceased*) friend P., and went with them to some place where they sat opposite each other as though they were at a small table. I sat in front of its narrow end. Fl. spoke about his sister and said that in three-quarters of an hour she was dead, and added some such words as 'that was the threshold.' As P. failed to understand him, Fl. turned to me and asked me how much I had told P. about his affairs. Whereupon, overcome by strange emotions, I tried to explain to Fl. that P. (could not understand anything at all because he) was not alive. But what I actually said – and I myself noticed the mistake – was '**Non vixit**.' I then gave P. a piercing look. Under my gaze he turned pale; his form grew indistinct and his eyes a sickly blue – and finally he melted away. I was highly delighted at this and I now realized that Ernest Fleischl, too, had been no more than an apparition, a 'revenant' ['ghost' – literally, 'one who returns']; and it seemed to me quite possible that people of that kind only existed as long as one liked or could be got rid of if someone wished it.[1]

In our earlier discussion we have noted the dream's revelation that Freud himself was under the spell of the past, and that at least in his unconscious he could receive ghostly visitors. Like Faust, Freud feels 'the spell of long-forgotten yearning …' as 'what had disappeared proves real,' (I, ll.25, 33).[2] Thus even in the dream itself, Freud's reason is not entirely asleep; he knew that the characters in the dream could be conjured up and dispensed with. Nonetheless I have noted that for Freud some of his old associations were so dear as well as so problematic that he was unwilling to dispense with them once and for all.

Now consider that Freud presides at the head of the table (the 'narrow end') where the father usually sits. The other two characters, one of whom is named Joseph in real life, sit opposite each other. Indeed Freud reported other associations to the dream, in which the figure of the Kaiser appears: a clear father surrogate. In this case the Kaiser was also named Josef and could stand for Freud's own rather glorious identification of himself with the Joseph of the Bible who triumphed over his brothers and became a master interpreter of others' dreams as well as of his own. Freud explains that his unconscious had selected men named Joseph as an allusion to the brother who is sent to Egypt, but he does not mention Joseph's fratricidal urges or those of his other brothers. Instead, Freud tells us: 'My own ego finds it very easy to hide itself behind the people of that name, since Joseph was the name of a man famous in the Bible as an interpreter of dreams.'[3]

The biblical Joseph indeed had been the victim of fratricidal impulses on the part of his brothers, who resented Joseph's claim to be a favorite of their father. Clearly Freud is here on the familiar territory of the brothers who, having eliminated the father, seek to do away with anyone of their own number who aspires to be the leader and to assume the mantle of patriarchal authority. However, it is easier in the dream for these fratricidal impulses to be represented by dead colleagues and friends, than it is for Freud to 'own' them as his own. Nonetheless, as I noted in Chapter 6, in the dream itself Freud does imagine that he can give a withering gaze to P. and eliminate him. The dream gives away the secret, so to speak, of Freud's own murderous impulses.

Furthermore, the 'dead' in this dream are those who had aroused Freud's jealousy during an earlier period of his life and who were, so to speak, his previous psychological victims. Freud's active imagination had consigned them to the grave for various offenses that reminded him of his own, for example, the desire to eliminate rivals and take the place of senior colleagues. These figures, then, were the characters of Freud's own private hell: people whose passions, like his own, seemed to be murderous, undying, and worthy of judgement, but people to whom he was nevertheless attached by bonds of affection that would not let them go.

Since Freud's dream-figures are shades, insubstantial reminders of his own fratricidal and patricidal impulses, we need not be surprised to find them representing Freud's old failings. In this dream, Freud had imagined the death of his friends in order to punish them for their ambition: an ambition, of course, that was like his own. In this respect they were imaginary surrogates for himself and his own desires. Hence the dream is like Freud's definition of child-play, hiding the self in others so as to act out and then to punish those alienated parts of the self.[4] Indeed, one occasion for the dream may have been Freud's recent attendance at a ceremony honoring the memory of Ernst Fleischl Von Marxow, an older colleague of Freud's at the Vienna Physiological Institute who had died seven years before.[5] Fleischl had been a dear friend of Freud's as well as a senior colleague whose position Freud understandably would have wanted for himself. Freud is quite candid about feeling both hostility and affection toward his colleagues, and so 'the late' Fleischl in the dream had not only died but also had been annihilated in Freud's fantasies, as had his friend P. whom Freud refers to as 'deceased' and who in real life was Josef Paneth: another representative of the victimized and victorious Joseph-figure with whom Freud had identified.[6] The funeral occasion could well have triggered not only memories of his loss but feelings of satisfaction at having triumphed at last over one older rival, as over a father: feelings for which Freud would have had reason to reproach himself, as he does in this dream. Certainly Freud thought that the primitive, repressed aspects of the psyche tend to return under certain conditions: the relaxation of controls, as during sleep; the strengthening of old impulses; and a recent event that triggers old memories and excites old passions.

We are now in a better position to understand why Freud thought that the biblical tradition carried with it reminiscences of patricide and fratricide. In the Hebrew Bible, indeed, these sins are punished by a father-God who, in the person of Moses and the tradition of Ikhnaton, returns as a monotheistic force for the higher impulses, an incentive to repression of murderous desires, and a continuing condemnation of the unbridled ego. These repressions, Freud thought, enabled the Jewish people to attain a higher level of civilization than could be achieved when the primitive returned, as it did under the auspices of the Christian Church, in the form of the rebellion of the Son against the Father. Although the Son clearly dies for his pretensions, he is resurrected in the sure and certain hope of a fraternal triumph at the end of history.

This sort of fantasy, in which the unconscious turns the tables on the reality-principle, allows magical thinking to return without the usual censorship provided by a patriarchal religion. Of course, the magical thinking is disguised in terms of biblical mythology. Joseph is the classical hero of the displaced self: originally removed from the scene, but eventually triumphant over rivals and in full possession of 'the field.' Indeed, Freud later remarks that, at the death of another friend (P., in the dream) he had found some satisfaction at being 'left in possession of field.'[7] Thus patricidal and fratricidal struggles in the dream are relatively clear and unremarkable, and behind them loom the struggles of earlier infancy to remove all competition for parental affection.

The search for the primitive self in Freud's interpretation of this dream, however, goes much further than these ambitions and fantasies of young adulthood and late adolescence. Freud points out that his later competitiveness was rooted in struggles with a nephew, who was in fact older than Freud, for full possession of the family field.[8] Perhaps even more to the point, he imagines a childhood scene in which both he and John claim to have '*got there before the other*': a phrase which Freud himself places in italics.[9] Their antagonism clearly had to do with their rival claims to possess a thing or a place. The womb, certainly, is just such a place where rival claims to sole possession and occupancy are resolved in favor of seniority. John was Freud's senior, because he was older, whereas Freud could claim to have been the senior as John's uncle. Thus the dead come back, and old psychological injuries and failings are relived: a necessary encounter with the past if the primitive self is, finally, to be recovered and to dissipate.

It is this primitive self, however, that adopts the later disguises of adulthood. The references in the dream to later conflict with his friends and colleagues '... screened with *their* affect the affect which arose from the forbidden infantile source.'[10] Thus Freud hides his infantile self, as he later points out, behind the adult characters. Freud's own self is further displaced by these 'late' colleagues whom he has internalized; they represent aspects of himself with which he is at odds. However, they are also former colleagues whom he has internalized 'and could be got rid of if someone wished it.' Indeed, as I noted in Chapter 6, the dream may have served the purpose of reassuring Freud that he could be purged of these unwanted presences in his psyche. One might say that in this dream Freud is not only imagining himself as catching up with those who have gone before but also as being able to put them behind, in the past, once and for all.

The yearning to recover the primitive self thus opens the door to a certain chronic form of guilt, since the primitive self is often engaged in such mental crimes and atrocities as fratricide and patricide. Some of these early, imaginary crimes, however, are sins of omission. For instance, in interpreting this dream, Freud reported that he was terribly worried at the time that his friend, Fliess, might be dying in a Berlin hospital: 'I must have imagined that ... I should make the journey after all – and arrive *too late*, for which I might never cease to reproach myself' (italics in the original).[11] As we have seen, Freud sees in this fear a veiled form of the wish to outlast all his friends and colleagues: a wish for the narcissistic triumph of having the field to himself, as it were.[12] Hence the need to reproach himself is a punishment for the crime of having taken secret satisfaction in having imagined that he had superceded others. The keen apprehension of being late, in the combined senses of being dead as well as tardy, would be a fitting psychological punishment for the imaginary crime of eliminating others in the struggle for exclusive access to the sources of life. Here the search for the primitive self has taken him again into psychological territory full of active magical thinking.

There are other games afoot here than magical thinking and infantile strivings for exclusive possession. We have seen that Freud, in discussing his thoughts about failing to arrive in Berlin before his friend, Fliess, should die, says that had he been too late he 'would never cease to reproach himself.'[13] Although we may never fully understand the reproach, we have yet to grasp why such self-condemnation would have had to be ceaseless. Freud is obviously ruminating about his need to catch up with those who have gone before: those whom he has lost to death or to other forms of drastic separation. In fact, a few pages later, Freud acknowledges that, about the time of this dream, he had been ruminating about how he had lost friendships, whether because of someone's death or through some fault, perhaps, of his own.[14] Reflecting on his train of thought during the 'ceremonial unveiling of the memorial' to his friend and colleague Fleischl, the one whose position had been so coveted by Josef Paneth (the 'P.' in the dream), Freud remembers thinking:

> 'What a number of valued friends I have lost, some through death, some through a breach of our friendship! How fortunate that I have found a substitute for them and that I have gained one who means more to me than ever the others could, and that, at a time of life when new friendships cannot easily be formed, *I shall never lose his*!' (emphasis added)[15]

*Ceaseless* reproach, then, is a fitting punishment for having imagined that one would have a friendship which transcends and triumphs over time: 'I shall never lose his!'[16]

Thus the dream expresses in a variety of ways Freud's own concern with the death of the soul. Its death is coded, of course, in terms of time; it is being 'late' that stands for being mortified or, finally, dead. Thus the fear of being late, in the several senses of the word, may have reflected Freud's desire not only to avoid death, in the literal sense, but also to prevent the premature death of the psyche itself. To be late in the sense of lacking seniority in the birth order; to be late in the sense of not being in time to be present before someone dies; to be late in the sense of harboring the ghost of

– or being identified with – a dead friend or relative; to be late because one identifies with the victims of one's own psychological crimes; and to be late in the sense of being reduced to 'nothing' by another's overwhelming presence: all these reflect Freud's fundamental concern with preventing the death of the soul. Like Dante, Freud can pity the moribund soul.

However, the attempt to recover the primitive psyche opens the door not only to chronic longing and guilt but to the confusion of multiple desires. Consider the polymorphous and perverse forms of love that Freud found in his own and others' childhood. For instance, while interpreting the dream we have just discussed, Freud goes on to associate Fliess's younger sister (who had died so abruptly in the dream) with the young sister of his nephew, John: '... the little girl I used to play with as a child, who was of my age and the sister of my earliest friend and opponent.'[17] She was part of what Freud earlier referred to as 'the ideal situation of childhood,' in which he and his friend-nephew John were both 'intimate' and 'inseparable' as well as frequent antagonists. With his nephew John, Freud had also imagined that here was a friendship that would go on forever. Before the reality-principle sets in and the rule of the father is affirmed in the depths of one's psyche, one can mix emotions freely, love incestuously, disregard gender limitations on the scope and objects of affection, and imagine that such love will go on forever.

Thus it was not surprising to Freud to discover that his unconscious was filled with magical thinking or that his psyche was host to 'revenants': to people who come back. The primitive often returns in the form of ghosts and demons. The point is that these ghosts were lost aspects of Freud's more primitive self, and that even in his dreams Freud was still at some pains to prevent the death of the soul even when it was too late to do so.

The journey to recover the primitive self and to revive the moribund levels of the psyche is never going to be smooth sailing and may even be perilous. One may undertake it with simplicity and courage, or with the histrionics of Goethe's imaginary Faust:

> Excitement, poignant happiness, love-hate,
> quickening frustration – to these I'm consecrated!
> Henceforth my heart, cured of its thirst for knowledge, will welcome
>     pain and suffering
> and I'm resolved my inmost being
> shall share in what's the lot of all mankind,
> that I shall understand their heights and depths,
> shall fill my heart with all their joys and griefs,
> and so expand myself to theirs
> and, like them, suffer shipwreck too,

I, ll.1766–1775[18]

Freud would have no quarrel, I believe, with Faust's intention to suffer ordinary passions or never to prolong a particular pleasure. Indeed, he shared the Faustian intention to '... plunge into the torrents of time/ into the whirl of eventful existence!' (I, ll.1754–1755):[19]

> If I should ever say to any moment
>     Tarry, remain! – you are so fair!
> then you may lay your fetters on me,
> then I will gladly be destroyed!
> Then they can toll the passing bell,
> your obligations then be ended –
> the clock may stop, its hand may fall,
> and time at last for me be over!
>
> I, ll.1699–1706[20]

You will remember that Mephistopheles did tell Faust that the clock had stopped precisely when Faust had begun to rest on his laurels for having preserved the lowlands from the sea.

Freud, too, disliked poetic regrets that time makes all pleasures temporary; it is time that heals memory and makes the fleeting moment sweet precisely because it is so evanescent. However, he would not have accepted Faust's reliance on magical thinking or his pursuit of unending pleasure. These indicated that Faust was not yet ready to give time its due and to accept its, and his own, irrevocable passage. Note that Faust refuses to surrender a certain amount of magical thinking; he exhorts Mephistopheles: 'May your magic be ready at anytime/to show me miracles whose veil cannot be lifted!' (I, ll.1752–1753).[21] Rather than lose his magical defense against running out of time, Faust is willing to risk his 'inmost being' in his relationship to Mephistopheles, as evidenced in the contract that is signed in his own blood. In his reliance on miracles or on divine rescue, there is thus a sacrifice of his essence: an echo of the self-destruction that Faust earlier had been contemplating as he considered the possibility of drinking from the vial of poison in his study. As I have argued, reliance on magical thinking or on fantasies of divine intervention are self-destructive residues not only of infancy but of early Christian asceticism.

By way of contrast, the secular, psychoanalytic descent into 'the torrents of time' renounces magical thinking and any thought of rescue; one's 'inmost being' is not to be sacrificed for the sake of an imaginary victory over time and its limits. Psychoanalysis is the end not only of romantic attempts to recover the primitive self but also of the monastic dream of a journey to spiritual perfection that relies wholly on divine assistance and final rescue.

The secular descent into hell under psychoanalytic auspices never renounces the autonomy of the innermost self; it eschews magical thinking, and acknowledges that no relationship endures beyond death, no matter what calisthenics and contortions the soul may engage in to preserve itself from the experience of intimate loss. To be sure, Freud in his youth believed, as does Faust, that certain friendships were supposed never to run out of time. Because Freud's friendships, first with his nephew John and later with Fliess, seemed to capture an important part of his inner self and were filled with mixed emotion, they were supposed to last forever. Like Faust's pact with Mephistopheles, they were a guarantee that he would never himself be 'late' (in the double sense of being not only tardy but dead). Ostensibly based on a desire to live life to the utmost, these eternal friendships were a covert bargain and sacrifice: a surrender of the inner self in order to gain protection against the passage of time and against death itself.

The Faustian project, like the Freudian, is an attempt to recover those parts of the self that have been split-off, denied, suppressed, or invested in another, through whom one henceforth lives vicariously. The difference between the two projects is that the Faustian seeks to immerse one in time and passion precisely in order to beat time at its own game: an attempt never to reach the point at which one is either too late or has had enough. Faust thus promises himself that he will live life to the utmost, but it is a promise that he cannot fulfill, having surrendered his inner autonomy to Mephistopheles. Faust is like an analysand who keeps being analyzed in order to discover ever more passion, ever more anguish, and to recover ever more of past longings and desire, ostensibly in a search for more original vitality, but actually in an attempt never to reach a limit or an end.

Like Freud, Goethe knows that the self is also filled with passionate strivings: greed, hunger, anger, rage, panic and all the other residues of infancy. Goethe's Faust, like Freud, knows that the self is not simply a transcendent and undisturbed nodal point from which one can observe the world in serenity; indeed Faust rejects serenity and abstraction for the life of passion and of the moment. This romantic journey departs from the secular descent into hell, however, in Faust's imagining that he can experience these without encountering any limits: no end to love, and no personal limitation on what he can endure.

I have been suggesting that the devil is a disguise of the father-figure, the one who knows the limits of human striving and who understands fully the passage of time. As I have noted, Mephistopheles indeed knows something about Faust's limits that Faust himself wishes to ignore: that '… even if he had no contract with the devil,/ he'd end up ruined anyhow!' (I, ll.1866–1867).[22] Faust's illusions about the passage of time have no place in a psychoanalytic descent into the unconscious to recover the soul.

To be sure, there are also analytic descents that go wrong; that is, they seem to go on indefinitely precisely because the one being analysed refuses to mark and accept the passage of time. The analysand may imagine that his or her relation to the analyst will never have an end; there will always be more analytical work to do: 'If on a bed of sloth I ever lie contented/ may I be done for then and there,' (I, ll.1692–1983).[23] As if expressing Faust's underlying wish, Mephistopheles assures him that 'You are not limited in any way,' (I, ll.1760).[24] In an interminable analysis one need never acknowledge that it is simply too late to satisfy old loves or avenge old injustices.

To those in grief for a friendship that was supposed to be undying, of course, the passage of time will be a source of disappointment and potential horror. Freud lamented such a loss, having enjoyed a friendship that was supposed, in his fantasies, to have been eternal. Like Faust and, perhaps, Dante, he had begun his project in grief and had found something terribly missing in the world. Such a grief understandably makes the world seem counterfeit; we have already noted Faust's lament that 'What I possess seems something far away/and what had disappeared proves real,' (I, ll.3133–3132).[25] To end such chronic sadness requires an act of the will: a decision to embrace the secular world in which time is continually passing away. Only such a decision to terminate the past can end the chronic attempt to find in this world something that is forever missing.

What is required is an act of will that renounces the search for the eternal. To elect the temporal, however, is to end once and for all one's rebellion against time rather than preserve any illusions of transcendence. For Faust such a renunciation is not unthinkable, but it is intolerable: 'But still our hearts have their illusions,/ and who would care to live without them?' (I, ll.1722–1723).[26] In the secular descent into hell, the renunciation of all such illusions about transcending the passage of time is an essential act of the will.

However, in reacting against the slow and partial death of the psyche the individual may seek a second merger of the soul: one that finally will protect the psyche from the erosion of time. On the journey to hell the psyche may thus imagine that it has once again found a relationship, like Dante's to Beatrice, and Faust's to The Queen of Heaven, that will transcend the passage of time. The secular descent into hell therefore requires the renunciation of the wish for a relationship that will take us beyond the barrier of death into a timeless love.

Such renunciation can be very difficult indeed. For instance, Freud's colleague, Salvador Ferenczi, noted that one of his patients had lost her 'sense of time:'

> The patient allowed letters to pile up over several months without opening them, believing there was plenty of time. As though time were suddenly something infinite, as though life did not have to come to an end in old age and death. At least not her life. In her analysis, therefore, the patient must be brought to suffer

from desires herself, instead of ensuring their absence with the help of imaginary identification.[27]

In Goethe's terms, she must plunge into the torrents of time and learn to suffer the ills that afflict the rest of mankind: experience them in her innermost being. That is why Ferenczi suggests that his patient should be helped once again to feel desire: to be aware that there remains a gap between the self and the ideal. She must give up her 'imaginary identification,' her tendency to fuse her own identity with some 'ready-made successful ideal of beauty or life:' a narcissistic victory over reality, at the price of the loss of the sense of her real self.[28] That is, he prescribed for her a psychoanalytic descent into hell, on the assumption that she would come to understand and accept the seal that time places on the satisfaction of desire.

The psychoanalytic descent is a long way from the monastic promise of divine intervention and rescue. It does not allow the believer to enshrine his or her own mortality in the context of a relationship that was the same yesterday, today, and forever. It offers no comfort to individuals and communities who seek to enclose their own stories, circumscribed by time, in a sacred history that begins before time and will end only after time itself has ceased.

The psychoanalytic journey, if completed, allows the will to terminate the past without the anesthetic of magic, encourages the psyche to recognize its limits without the illusion of transcendence, and requires the individual to face his or her own death without the comfort of a timeless love. The act of will to enter time on its own terms entails a renunciation of any longings to restore the primordial unity of the original matrix. By contrast, the Faustian journey to hell, like the monastic journey of Cassian, postpones confrontation with one's own limits and inevitable death. Each is a reaction-formation to the death of the psyche: to be sure, a defense against such psychic death, but one which puts the psyche once again into mortal jeopardy because the individual does not renounce illusion or magic and thus refuses to acknowledge that it is too late to fulfill ancient longings.

## Notes

1 Sigmund Freud (1965), *The Interpretation of Dreams*, New York: Avon Books (A Division of The Hearst Corporation), p. 456–7; underlining added.

2 Stuart Atkins (1984), *Goethe. The Collected Works*, Princeton, NJ: Princeton University Press, p. 1.

3 Freud, op. cit., p. 522.

4 The figures also represented other failings that Freud regretted. For instance, the appearance of Fliess represents the offense of revealing personal secrets (Freud recounts how he himself had felt rebuked when Fliess discovered that Freud had indiscreetly revealed personal details that Fliess had preferred to keep secret).

5 Freud, op. cit., p. 520, n. 1.
6 Freud, ibid., p. 459.
7 Ibid., p. 523.
8 Ibid., pp. 520 ff.
9 Ibid., p. 521.
10 Ibid., p. 523.
11 Ibid., pp. 518–19.
12 Freud arrives at this interpretation by recalling that it is Fliess whose sister, in the dream, had died rather abruptly.
13 Freud, op. cit., pp. 518–19.
14 Ibid., p. 523.
15 Ibid., pp. 523–624; emphasis added.
16 Ibid., p. 524.
17 Ibid.
18 Atkins, op. cit., pp. 45–6.
19 Ibid., p. 45.
20 Ibid., p. 44.
21 Ibid., p. 45.
22 Ibid., p. 48.
23 Ibid., p. 44.
24 Ibid., p. 45.
25 Ibid., p. 1.
26 Ibid., p. 44.
27 Ferenczi, Sándor, *The Clinical Diary of Sándor Ferenczi*, edited by Judith Dupont, translated by Michael Balint and Nicola Zarday Jackson (1988), Cambridge, Mass. and London, England: Harvard University Press, p. 142.
28 Ibid.

# Chapter 9

# The Secular Pilgrim's Progress
# Through Hell

I have been arguing for the recovery of the notion of a secularized descent into hell, in which the psychoanalytic tradition completes and corrects the Christian religious and secular, scriptural and literary, legacy. Certainly, as the philosopher Thomas J.J. Altizer put it, 'damnation and Hell dominate the New Testament as they do no other scripture in the world.'[1] Not only was the descent into hell a part of the Christian Creed known as the Nicaean. It was essential to the Gospel itself. Indeed, some elements of the Christian community understood the mission of Jesus to have begun at a moment of resistance to temptation by the devil and to continue as Jesus liberates individuals from their pasts. Often he encounters those who believe that it is too late for those whom they love to be healed or rescued, although their desire lives on; he demonstrates that in his presence it is not too late and that time has not yet run out. It is as if Jesus is harrowing the hell in which the early Christian community lived.

As Altizer puts it, to undertake the descent into hell is 'to be awakened to the ultimacy of the human condition.'[2] He goes on to say that

> ... if the way 'up' for us is inevitably the way 'down' then we can know only a Jesus who has descended into Hell, and not a Jesus who has ascended into Heaven. To know another Jesus would be to know a Jesus who has no actual point of contact with us, yet to know a Jesus who has descended into Hell would be to know a Jesus who is incarnate for us.[3]

To make the descent into hell is to renounce the desire for a transcendent moment that contains and fulfills, yet supercedes, all that has gone before. Precisely such a renunciation is contained in the narratives of the temptation of Christ. As Peter Salm points out, moreover, it is the devil who offers to give Jesus

> 'All the kingdoms of the world in a moment of time' – this moment, a pinprick, translated from the Greek *stigme chronou*, is the most irresistible gift offered to man. In both Luke and Goethe's *Faust*, it is offered by the devil and is illicit because it usurps the prerogative of divinity.[4]

Here again is the devil, as the combination of the father-figure and of rebellion against patriarchal authority, who offers a short cut to the privileges of patriarchy, chief among which is transcendence over the passage of time.

Thus it is within the intention of the gospel writers, at least of Luke from whom this temptation story is taken, to suggest that the life of Christ was a refusal to enter into a (Faustian) compromise with the devil. Jesus would encounter pure temporality without the comforts of eternity. That is why his final temptation is in the Garden of Gethsemane, where he continues to experience the longing for life, even while knowing that it is too late. Although he prays 'Take this cup from me,' he nevertheless submits to the divine will that his time should be finished. Faust, by way of contrast, puts the cup of death aside and searches for a moment of transcendence over time, even while insisting that he wishes nothing more than to experience life on its own temporal terms.

The search for moments that last forever is like the poet's attempt at transcending the agony of the pilgrim, an elusive and incomplete sort of transcendence. That search for transcendence is bound to fail, even or especially if it is undertaken by Christian theologians. Take this telling criticism by John Freccero:

> Augustine's journey to God, like Dante's, is immediately preceded by a journey that fails, an attempt at philosophical transcendence in the seventh book of the *Confessions* that amounts to a conversion manquee ... The Platonic conversion toward the light is doomed to failure because it neglects to take account of man's fallen condition. To put the matter in Platonic terms, the pilgrim must struggle even to reach the cave from which Plato assumed the journey began.[5]

Whereas the Gospels describe a world in which the ultimate is caught up in the momentary, both Dante and Goethe were describing the search for a moment that lasts forever, and for an eternity in which everything occurs simultaneously. More is required for the descent into hell, moreover, than courage and insight. One must also have a will stronger than one's passions; otherwise one will surrender oneself to these primitive longings and be unable to return to the world above. Lacking the will to relegate those passions to the past, those in hell remain caught up in old loves and battles; even while knowing that it is entirely too late for them to alter the past, their will remains captivated by old desire. The souls in hell continue to suffer, even though they know that there is nothing that can be done to resolve or consummate these old passions or to undo old crimes. As Freud said of the libido, there is no passage of time, and the libido acts as if it had a will of its own that persists even when the time for fulfillment has long since passed away. Thus Freud would have understood Dante's description of the will embedded in the wishes that refuse to dissipate over time:

O blind desire /
Of covetousness, O anger gone insane – /
That goad us on through life, which is so brief, /
To steep in eternal woe when life is done,

Canto XII.42–44[6]

There is thus a danger for the living if they are to follow Dante's footsteps into the psyche and seek to recover the past. They may lack the will eventually to turn their back upon the past. The psychoanalytic equivalent of such a fate would be an interminable analysis, in which the analysand knows that it is too late to do anything about old fears and fantasies but nevertheless continues to experience them as active possibilities in the present.

If it were not the presence of a trained guide like Virgil, Dante himself, as pilgrim in hell, indeed might not have been able to abandon his fascination with the past. To return to the world in which the living are fully engaged in the present requires an act of the will. Otherwise one is immersed in the libido, just as souls in hell are pictured by Dante as being literally covered, even swamped, by blood and mire. These are libidinous images, and they effectively convey the work of the libido in erasing any experience of the passage of time. So pressing are the emotions that belong to the past that both progress through hell and a return to the land of the living are possible only for those who willfully put the past behind them.

Such an act of the will is difficult, especially for those for whom the past, like the libido itself, continues to exercise a certain fascination. The libido, as I have noted, is impervious to the passage of time. As one traverses the psychic territory of the past, one's reason must therefore take the role of Virgil, who performs that function for Dante by looking at the stars. Indeed, it is usually up to Virgil to warn Dante about the passage of time. For instance, when Dante begins to ask Virgil to look back at the first circles of hell, Virgil asks Dante, 'What brings/Your thoughts to wander so far from the proper route?' (Canto XI.75–76).[7] The 'proper route,' of course is forward into the further depths of hell. As if to point out that Dante's regressive inquiry has cost them some time, the Canto closes with Virgil's observation that it is getting late.

If one is to enter into the experience of 'hell' one must therefore renounce any sort of remorseful nostalgia. A secular descent offers no license to satisfy longings that are clearly dated and whose time, so to speak, has long expired. The refusal to accept the fact that the time has long since past in which it would have been possible to fulfill certain aspirations or satisfy certain desires keeps old parts of the self alive that could have been allowed to disappear. In such a state, there is no way for the self to enter into the present. That way opens only to those who know and experience the fact that it is too late to satisfy primitive longings even though these longings persist in their original form and intensity.

Moreover, this search is often hidden under an apparent willingness to embrace temporality. However, Peter Salm makes the point that Faust's journey would be over if ever he surrendered to the desire for a total victory over the temporal: 'an all-encompassing moment of existence.' We know that in the end Faust succumbs to just such a desire to transcend the momentary.[8] Let us therefore take a last look at Faust. Displaced from the embrace of nature, in agony over the loss of his youthful, infantile self, in despair of being able to recover and control what eludes his grasp, and with the rage of the infant longing for a maternal presence that its cries can no longer summon and command, Faust vows 'to ban the shore to the imperious sea' and demands the devil's help in building dikes (II, ll.10,229–233).[9] The dikes become the angry adult's version of the infantile hands that failed to grasp and control the maternal breasts. If one cannot own and control the primitive forces that give us birth, we will create a surrogate world of our own.

Faust is driven, however, by an awareness that it is too late to recover the original vision and thus too late to recover the vital, animated soul that was present at the beginning. Mephisotopheles had already asked Faust, 'what's gotten into you/ and made you land amid the horror/of these hideous maws of rock?' (II, ll.10,068–070).[10] The rock, Mephistopheles goes on to say, 'once paved the floor of hell' but, after volcanic eruptions from the gaseous underworld, erupted and now floors the world above. Hell, in other words, has become this worldly, and the netherworld has come, so to speak, to the surface of social life.

Faust is having none of this revelation, however; he wishes to believe in the perfection of nature and the perfectibility of the world. Thus Faust goes on to dream of holding back the sea with well-constructed dikes that, like the mountains themselves, would restrain the tides and provide a sanctuary on earth for the human community: safe from aimless, repetitive and destructive tidal forces: safe from the primitive that was the initial object of Faust's journey. Mother Nature would no longer be able to come and go at her own pleasure but would remain at Faust's command.

What Faust, as the secular pilgrim personified, cannot stand is the sight of the 'aimless strength of elemental forces' that accomplish nothing and remain beyond his control. In despair over grasping 'the breasts of Infinite Nature,' he resolves 'to wage war here against these forces and subdue them,' (II, ll.10,216–221).[11] Thus Faust's well-intended pathway, as it were, is now paved with the rocks of hell. Having lost his original soul, the one that thrived in the enchanted world of the infant, he is seeking a surrogate soul through action. He would like 'to rule and have possessions! Acts alone count – glory is nothing,' (II, ll.10,187–188).[12] This indeed became a fascist mantra of deeds over words or other imaginary actions. Like the fascists themselves, he is now seeking to create a civil order that cannot be washed away by the tides of nature and history. It is such a fantasy that seals Faust's fate; at the moment that Faust imagines that he can indeed transcend the passage of time, he dies and thus becomes truly 'late.'

It is through this secular pilgrimage into the passage of time that one will recover a Jesus exposed to and even embodying the passage of time. Such a secular pilgrimage, however, requires an equally radical secularization of the Christian religion as it is currently understood and practiced by the churches of our own time. That is also why, in the preceding chapters, I have been arguing that the primitive has returned under Christian auspices, but that it has not been sufficiently acknowledged and understood as the primitive. Work remains to be done to expunge from the Christian tradition the vestiges of magical thinking and grandiose imagination, the remains of old grievances and the longing for ultimate triumph, that make that tradition toxic to the psyche and occasionally dangerous to social peace and justice.

Thus it is inauthentic to take a descent into hell as the first step on a spiritual journey when arrival at the destination is guaranteed from the beginning, while those in hell are already at the end of their road. To be sure, there is a pilgrimage through the depths of passion and despair that must be taken if the soul is ever to arrive on firm ground in clear possession of a vision of the end of human life and history. For the convert and the poet, as for the philosopher, it is easier to pursue a course toward a mountain bathed in light than to descend to the depth of human experience; no doubt the choice of the higher course toward enlightenment is a result of a failure of the will to be humbled, after the manner of Christ in becoming human.[13]

If, however, the secular pilgrimage into hell is aborted or fails, and if attempts to transcend the passage of time philosophically leave one poised like Icarus for a deadly fall, it is no wonder that the earlier, more primitive and vigorous self demands a second chance. Remember the Faustian attempt to lay hold of the sources of life: Goethe's return to the primitive. To get one's hands on the elemental forces of the universe, as on the mother herself, is the underlying goal of the primitive self. Even when that energy is transformed into productive and rational activity, the underlying motive is the narcissistic striving to own and control the sources of life. The spring to any action, especially productive work, is thus coiled around magical thinking and regressive impulse: the primitive itself.

To offset the effect of religious and romantic temporizing, therefore, I have been arguing that in hell the passage of time is irreversible. The secular descent into hell is an encounter with primitive passions, but with the knowledge that it is therefore forever too late to fulfill such desires and longings, however much they may continue to persist in unmitigated intensity. It is an encounter with the irreversible and irrevocable passage of time. Note the absence not only of any romantic notions of making up for lost time but of any religious certainty of divine rescue. One is left with a Christian faith that urges the individual to 'let the dead bury the dead,' to abandon traditional obligations, to subordinate ritualized observances to the needs of the moment, and to replace pious waiting with insistence on readiness at all times and places to make the most of opportunities for wholeness. The ministry of Jesus thus constituted a radical secularization of the religious institutions and practices of his own time, and to recover such a Jesus would require a similarly radical secularization of Christian faith and practice in our own times.

The realm of the underworld in the psyche is full of passions that cannot be satisfied in any civil society, and it is full of longings that, even in a decent community, are seldom fulfilled. Obviously, the secular pilgrimage into the netherworld of the psyche asks a great deal of communities that may view animal spirits with alarm or of any society that enshrines and attracts the most grandiose and destructive of human emotions to the shrines of its own national devotions. However, the excluded aspects of the psyche often contain the truth about human nature that any society must know if it is not itself to be deluded, and it contains reservoirs of creativity and affection without which any society will soon stagnate. As for individuals, the path to the soul inevitably lies through a recovery of long-postponed desires and painful memories, if only so they can be finally discarded. There is nothing new in these assumptions, of course. Such a journey to the spiritual underworld used to be part of a religious tradition that employed dreams and visions to personify the cast of characters that plays itself out in the depths of the psyche but that also has counterparts among priests and bishops, princes and kings.

The secular pilgrimage into the psychic underworld will uncover not only the depths of what is uniquely personal but also experiences and symbols that are irreducibly social in nature. It is in the psyche that one comes alive to – or suppresses – the meaning and impact of one's social experience, just as it is in social life that one often acts out the aspirations and longings of the unconscious. Thus, as we have seen, Christian ascetics, visionaries and poets have long understood the psychic underworld as the place that one had to go if one were to possess one's own soul. In that journey, however, one meets not only very primitive parts of the self in a variety of disguises but a wide range of social actors: angels and demons, old friends and enemies, strangers who seem familiar, and familiar faces that seem a bit strange.

To descend into this spiritual netherworld is to experience hopeless longing. In the psychological state of hell, one knows that one cannot go back to the infantile state of relative bliss, recover lost lovers, satisfy old grievances, undo one's own past, and recover parts of the psyche that have been split off and can be known only in their manifold disguises. Indeed, it may be too late to recover parts of the self that, having been repressed, have finally died. One cannot resurrect the part of the self that died in a moment of ecstasy or fright, of humiliation or exalted fantasy, just as one cannot recover someone who has died.

Fears that one's soul may be dying often are transformed into a preoccupation with time. For instance, an emotion that is too strong to be borne may perhaps be silenced and split off. That part of the self then begins to die and contributes to the experience of the self as being chronically late: the term 'late' applying equally to the experience of missed opportunity and psychic death. Moreover, longing to be in the presence of an old love becomes transformed into a fear that one is running late. To descend into such a psychic hell is thus both a trip into one's interior depths and an encounter with the temporal limits of human existence. Indeed, the critical encounter with those limits comes when one knows that it is too late to satisfy a longing still so intense that life itself seems to require its fulfillment.

It is necessary, I have been suggesting, to revive the longstanding Christian tradition of a descent into hell in search for the psyche but also to revise it under the auspices of psychoanalytic criticism. However, I do not mean to suggest that the Christian tradition keep open the possibility that the past can be resurrected or re-enacted. Magical games with time include the notion that the future can be not only anticipated but inaugurated by symbolic action rather than by the hard work of abandoning cherished parts of the soul to the past once and for all. The journey into the depths of one's own psyche requires rigorous and analytical self-inquiry, recognition and letting go.

Where the Christian tradition and psychoanalysis overlap and feed each other is in their common concern to prevent the death of the soul. Of course, some forms of psychic death are necessary and desirable. Those we love do die, and to continue to search for them, as Dante searched for Beatrice after her death, is to condemn us to a romance with death itself. Individuals do grow up, and so to long for a return to the real as well as to the imaginary satisfactions of infancy and childhood is to enter into a hopeless war with reality itself. There is some truth in the religious insistence on conversion, if conversion means a frank willingness to discard parts of the self that ought to be moribund because they are outdated and stand in the way of further growth. The question is whether religious conversion requires the repression and splitting-off of parts of the self that do not fit an ideal image, rather than simply letting-go of the infantile and arrested parts of the soul. There is, in the secular descent into hell, a conversion to reality itself: a commitment to know and to understand the most primitive aspects both of the psyche and of social life.

It might seem that a secular descent into hell has no redemptive connotations. No longer reduced to a place in a scheme of salvation, hell has now become a framework for understanding the fate of passion in the passage of time. For instance, in his superb discussion of Rodin's sculpture, *The Gates of Hell*, Elsen quotes at length from Anatole France's article on that artist's vision of hell:

But Rodin's Hell no more resembles that of Dante than the thought of our time resembles that of the 13th century ...

There are no more demons, or at least the demons hide themselves inside the damned. The bad angels who cause the suffering of men and women are their passions, their loves and their hates, it is their flesh and their thoughts. These couples who pass 'so lightly on the wind' cry: Our eternal tormentors are within us. We carry within our selves the fire that burns us. Hell is the earth, it is human existence, it is the flight of time, it is the life during which one dies without cease. The Hell of the lovers is the desperate effort to put infinity in an hour, to stop life in one of their kisses which on the contrary announces the end; the Hell of the voluptuaries is the decadence of their flesh in the midst of eternal joy.

And I discover with sympathy that the Hell of Rodin is no longer a Hell of vengeances and that it is a Hell of tenderness and pity.[14]

Note the return of pity: that emotion against which Virgil warned Dante as being the foolish regard of the living for the hopeless dead. It is the emotion of the poet who takes the sting from hell by softening the confrontation not only with passion but with finality.

To some it might seem as if Rodin's sculpture marks the secularization of hell. For instance, Elsen points out that for many poets of the nineteenth century, hell was a secular condition for which there was no remedy: a 'Christianity without redemption and original sin without Christ ... Satan and sin had been secularized.'[15] For the romantic poets, as for Hugo and Baudelaire, in hell 'sorrow was queen'; it was up to the poet to emulate Hugo's God, who was an 'an infinite look into eternal sorrow.'[16] Perpetual mourning had been transformed by the poets into sorrowful regard.[17]

In extracting a spiritual discipline from romantic poets, therefore, one has to be careful to distinguish the poet from the true pilgrim. The poet understands the presence of the future and of the past within the present, and his or her horizons are thus vastly enlarged. For the poet the end is in sight, and the foreground is always therefore replete with meaning. For the pilgrim, each step along the way leaves the past further behind although the end is not yet in sight. The present and the passage of time offer no guarantees of spiritual elevation. The latter's journey is perilous and affords no transcendent perspective along the way. For the Dante scholar, John Freccero, the pilgrim is thus too immersed in the provisional and accidental, the temporary and the partial world of mundane experience, unlike *The Thinker* on top of Rodin's *The Gates of Hell*.[18] From the poet's view, the pilgrim can be sure of the destination and outcome of his spiritual journey or, conversely, of his hopeless immersion in the underworld.

The notion of the poet's elevated perspective is thus neither new or particularly modern. Standing on top of *The Gates of Hell* are his three shades: identical sculptures in positions that rotate about a pivotal point above the abyss beneath them, where Rodin's figures yearn after each other or suffer in self-contained anguish. Some seek to break the frames of the doors themselves and thus to emerge from the very portals of hell, while others seem barely able to emerge from their miasmic background. Rodin's hell is a theatre not only of perpetual mourning but of primitive, and therefore hopeless, passion.

Just below the three shades, however, and safely above the primitives below, is the figure of *The Thinker: The Poet*. As I have suggested, he is like the poet who imagines his pilgrimage into hell from the relative comfort of one who can transcend the passage of time. As John Freccero puts it:

> The pilgrim's view is much like our own view of history and of ourselves: partial, perhaps confused, still in the making. But the poet's view is far different, for it is global and comprehensive, the total view of a man who looks at the world, his neighborhood, and indeed himself with all the detachment of a cultural anthropologist.[19]

Like Rodin's *Thinker*, the poet's imaginative descent into hell may be recollected in such tranquility that the poet never enters the framework of despair. From the poet's viewpoint, the descent into hell may be merely a step on a journey: the beginning of a pilgrimage of the soul that ends, if not in beatitude, at least in exquisite sensibility. It is therefore never too late for the soul to feel passion. The poet's descent into hell is more like a Faustian immersion into the currents of time: a safe journey, since one's destination is a transfiguring vision, and that vision is guaranteed by the framework of the poem itself.

For the poet, I am arguing, it is not yet too late to recover the past. Take Rilke, for example:

> O longing for the places that weren't loved
> enough during the passing hour,
> that from afar I want to offer them
> the added act and the forgotten gesture
>
> Retrace my steps – this time alone –
> slowly make that journey over,
> remain by the fountain longer,
> touch that tree, caress this bench ...
>
> *Orchards*, no. 41[20]

The poet may retrace his or her steps under the guise of making spiritual progress. However, the need to imagine oneself as going back in time and satisfying the longing to love suggests that the inner self is enthralled by memory. The poet avoids the hell of knowing that it is too late by holding out the possibility of renewed spiritual connection with the past. It is never too late, whatever the passion, to find fulfillment. Thus Rilke goes on to imagine himself visiting a grave in silence:

> For hasn't it become essential
> to make a subtle, pious contact?
>
> *Orchards*, no. 41[21]

To face the present without being able to have a foretaste of the future or conjure up the past is an intolerable fate, but it belongs to others, not to the poet. Hopeless passion is there to be contemplated rather than endured. The poet's viewpoint is from a perch on top of *The Gates of Hell*. Consider these lines from Rilke:

> Tonight there was something in the air
> that makes us bow our heads;
> we want to pray for prisoners for whom life stops.
> And we think of life stopped ...
>
> Of life no longer moving towards death
> and of where the future's absent;
> where one must be uselessly strong
> and sad, uselessly.
>
> *Orchards*, no. 42[22]

The poet's elevated view of hell can be seen as Rilke goes on to describe the prison of the soul as a place 'Where all days are marking time, where all nights fall into the abyss,' because 'our heart's too old to think a child,' (*Orchards*, no. 42).[23] Some, like the prisoner, must be neither dead or alive; they are 'sad, uselessly.' Others, however, are not yet 'too old to think a child' and can make up for lost time through imagination. The primitive returns in the form of a child's imaginary ability to make up for lost time.

The poet's illusion is that one can actually go back in time to 'remain by the fountain longer, touch that tree, caress this bench.' It is never too late to imagine that one can retrace one's steps, to make 'the forgotten gesture,' or to establish 'a subtle, pious contact.' Those who think they are helpless to ward off the end of their time are deluded:

> It's not so much that life is hostile,
> but that we lie to it,
> locked in a block of immobilized fate,
>
> *Orchards*, no. 42[24]

That 'block of immobilized fate' indeed recalls Dante's hell, but it remains now for the poet to transform hell from a place of perpetual mourning into a place the sorrowful contemplation of which allows one to believe that one can retrace one's journey and, like the figure atop Rodin's *The Gates of Hell*, transcend the primitive even in the act of contemplating it. The poet, like Dante's souls in hell, may mourn the native city and grieve over being unable to return to the place of birth, but the poet also still believes in the possibility of making 'the forgotten gesture.' Contrast the soul in hell, who lacks any illusion about the possibility of transcending the passage of time.

Rilke's elevated perspective on 'immobilized fate' and on those who, like the prisoner, are 'sad, uselessly,' evokes the transcendent perspective of *The Thinker: The Poet*. Contrast the figures on *The Gates of Hell*, those primitives who are thoroughly driven by what Anatole France called the 'demons' that hide within us and the 'bad angels' that are our passions. Whatever glimpse of infinity is afforded *The Thinker: The Poet* by his perch above the morass of souls below, such a viewpoint is denied to those who are caught up in 'the flight of time.' Since it is too late for these damned souls to satisfy the longings that haunt them, they experience time as a reminder of all the loves they continue to cherish but have lost forever.

Had Freud been the contemplative figure above the portals, the figures on *The Gates of Hell* might well have represented the shades in his dreams: the ghostly figures and 'revenants' who, as Freud pointed out, were merely disguises for himself. They would not be merely the unhappy creatures of the poetic or religious imagination: vestiges of a former self that survive on 'subtle, pious contact' with oneself in the present. They would be oneself, disguised, perhaps, in a variety of other roles and personae, but nonetheless shades of one's own more primitive, unforgotten and still miserable self and personae that are familiar from the social encounters of everyday life.

The descent into hell thus requires more than a mere foray into the unconscious: the place where images of the self emerge from a miasma of recent experience and old memories, of daily arousal and subterranean passion. It requires more than a romance with death. It requires a renunciation of the desire to be restored to the vitality and security of the womb and of any sublimated attempt to recover the comforts of infancy. That means a willingness to live life in time on its own terms and to enter into the passage of time without guarantees of rescue, recovery or restoration. If there is ever to be an end to the madness that comes from scoring symbolic victories over time through various forms of human sacrifice, it will come from a secular encounter with the passage of time at the deepest levels of the psyche.

# Notes

1 Thomas J.J. Altizer (1997), *The Descent Into Hell: A Study of the Radical Reversal of the Christian Consciousness*, San Francisco: Harper, (1984) 1997, p. 191.
2 Ibid., p. 191.
3 Ibid., p. 198.
4 Peter Salm (1986), *Pinpoint of Eternity, European Literature in Search of the All-Encompassing Moment*, Lanham, New York, London: University Press of America, p. 70.
5 John Freccero, edited and with an introduction by Rachel Jacoff (1986), *Dante. The Poetics of Conversion*, Cambridge, Mass. and London, England: Harvard University Press, pp. 5, 9.
6 *The Inferno of Dante*. A New Verse Translation by Robert Pinsky (1996), New York, The Noonday Press, Farras, Straus and Giroux, p. 95.
7 Ibid., p. 89.
8 Salm, op. cit., p. 69.
9 Stuart Atkins (1984), *Goethe. The Collected Works*, Princeton, NJ: Princeton University Press, p. 25.
10 Ibid., p. 254.
11 Ibid., p. 258.
12 Ibid., p. 257.
13 Freccero, op. cit., p. 24.
14 Albert E. Elsen (1985), *The Gates of Hell, by Auguste Rodin*, Stanford, California: Stanford University Press, from Anatole France, 'La Porte de l'Enfer,' *L'Echo de Semaine* (Paris), June 17, 1900; p. 164.
15 Ibid., p. 228.
16 Elsen, *The Gates of Hell*; from Henry Peyre, *Victor Hugo: Philosophy and Poetry*, trans Roda P. Roberts, University of Alabama Press, 1980; 1985:228.
17 Note that Rodin once had entitled the contemplative figure above *The Gates of Hell* not merely *The Thinker* but *The Thinker: The Poet*; in doing so Rodin had left the door open to a wide range of interpretation. One of Rodin's biographers, implicitly comparing him to *The Thinker* on *The Gates of Hell*, writes that Rodin was '... walled in by his thoughts ... the need to educate himself had become an obsession.' As part of his self-education Rodin did steep himself in Dante, who, Cladel noted, 'struck his imagination like a hot iron,' but Rodin also read deeply in Virgil and Aeschylus, Shakespeare and Lamartine.
18 Freccero, op. cit., pp. 13–14, 4–5. Those of his contemporaries who imagined that Rodin's statue of *The Thinker* represented Dante himself presiding over Hell were therefore only partially right. Judith Clade (1950), *Rodin, sa vie glorieuse, sa vie inconnue*, Paris: Bernard Grasset, p. 84; Elsen, op. cit., p. 226.
19 Freccero, op. cit., p. 25.
20 *The Complete French Poems of Rainer Maria Rilke*, translated by A. Poulin, Jr. (1979), with a Foreword by W. D. Snodgrass, Saint Paul: Graywolf Press, p. 185.
21 Ibid.
22 Ibid.
23 Ibid., p. 187.
24 Ibid.

# Index